MONEY TALKS, BULLSH*T WALKS

INSIDE THE CONTRARIAN MIND
OF BILLIONAIRE MOGUL SAM ZELL

BEN JOHNSON

PORTFOLIO

PORTFOLIO
Published by the Penguin Group
Penguin Group (USA) Inc., 375 Hudson Street, New York, New York 10014, U.S.A.
Penguin Group (Canada), 90 Eglinton Avenue East, Suite 700, Toronto,
Ontario, Canada M4P 2Y3 (a division of Pearson Penguin Canada Inc.)
Penguin Books Ltd, 80 Strand, London WC2R 0RL, England
Penguin Ireland, 25 St Stephen's Green, Dublin 2, Ireland
(a division of Penguin Books Ltd)
Penguin Books Australia Ltd, 250 Camberwell Road, Camberwell,
Victoria 3124, Australia (a division of Pearson Australia Group Pty Ltd)
Penguin Books India Pvt Ltd, 11 Community Centre, Panchsheel Park,
New Delhi–110 017, India
Penguin Group (NZ), 67 Apollo Drive, Rosedale, North Shore 0632,
New Zealand (a division of Pearson New Zealand Ltd)
Penguin Books (South Africa) (Pty) Ltd, 24 Sturdee Avenue,
Rosebank, Johannesburg 2196, South Africa

Penguin Books Ltd, Registered Offices:
80 Strand, London WC2R 0RL, England

First published in 2009 by Portfolio,
a member of Penguin Group (USA) Inc.

1   3   5   7   9   10   8   6   4   2

LIBRARY OF CONGRESS CATALOGING-IN-PUBLICATION DATA
Johnson, Ben, 1960-
Money talks, bullsh-t walks : inside the contrarian mind of billionaire mogul Sam Zell /
Ben Johnson.
p. cm.
Includes bibliographical references and index.
ISBN 978-1-59184-300-9
1. Zell, Sam, 1941-   2. Capitalists and financiers—United States—Biography.
3. Real estate developers—United States—Biography.   I. Title.
HG172.Z45J66 2009
333.3092—dc22
[B]   2009037204

Printed in the United States of America
Set in Fairfield Light
Designed by Victoria Hartman

This book is dedicated to my loving wife, Angela,
adoring daughter, Alex, and constant companion, Sophie,
for their patience in seeing me through the
long days and nights when it was "all about me."
And to my mom and dad for their many sacrifices along
the way to ensure my brother and I had a leg up.
I just hope they're all proud.

CONTENTS

MONEY TALKS, BULLSH*T WALKS

PROLOGUE

IT WAS NO way to start the workweek, especially for one of the richest people in the world, with a net worth of $3 billion. But after a long and painful weekend spent haggling with many of the world's largest banking institutions, Samuel Zell knew his options had run out. Early on the morning of Monday, December 8, 2008, the noted Chicago investor was putting the finishing touches on the bankruptcy filing for his Tribune Company, the third-largest media conglomerate in America.

This move would mark the largest blemish on his stunningly successful forty-five-year business career. But with almost $13 billion in debt killing the company, even Zell, one of the most prescient and successful modern-day investors, had no tricks left up his sleeve.

Coming after less than a year under Zell's ownership—353 days to be precise—Tribune's demise quickly became the largest media bankruptcy in history. And for Zell, it was an uncharacteristic, and high profile, failure. After all, he was one of history's greatest contrarian investors, a respected firebrand of a titan who had elevated himself by his bootstraps: parlaying a puny $1,500 real estate invest-ment into billions in personal wealth.

Throughout the 1970s, '80s and '90s, Zell's business track record had become the stuff of legend, marked by spectacular bits of mar-ket timing and a penchant for going against the grain. His primary strategy was to scarf up troubled companies on the cheap, then rely on his management skills and intuition to turn them around. Later he would sell them off for a bundle. He also became known for his prickly demeanor and blunt, no-bullshit style. Though he often spoke in braggadocious terms, he nearly always backed up his mouth with results.

Through success and failure, Zell became the quintessential poster child for contrarianism. He revels in the passion of life, suck-ing every last nickel and dime out of it, in business and in pleasure. As he put it, "I challenge conventional wisdom and I continually test my limits."[1]

What really sealed Zell's stellar reputation was one whopper of a deal. In February 2007, he sold his Equity Office Properties Trust, the largest owner of office buildings in the world, for a hefty $39 bil-lion to Blackstone Group. That was the largest leveraged buyout in corporate history (at the time) and more important, was executed at the absolute peak of the real estate market bubble. Certainly Zell's sale was a prescient one, as he narrowly escaped the looming real estate industry collapse and subsequent panic in the global financial system in the latter stages of 2007 and 2008.

But just as Zell reached the absolute pinnacle of his career, his entrepreneurial nature would not allow him to sit contentedly on his billions in Equity winnings. Instead he remained true to his risk-taking nature. In a cruel twist of irony, he was eying a new prize—Tribune—on the very same day he was cashing out on the Equity Office sale.

Though Zell had shown a penchant for the offbeat when it came to investing—making a fortune in unglamorous industries, including cargo containers, fertilizer, and even plumbing—publishing was one business sector he had not tapped with his billions. Still, to the consummate turnaround artist and "vulture" investor, it represented one of the highest mountains yet to climb. Zell is a voracious deal maker, constantly scanning the headlines for his next prey. He knows that most troubled companies can be steered successfully through their crises, if the right management structure and talent can be brought to bear on the situation.

With Tribune, though, Zell pushed well past his limits. No amount of timing or judicious use of four-letter words—which Zell tosses around more frequently than radio shock jock Howard Stern—could save his hide. There was no getting past the harsh reality that this deal was done at the worst possible moment, just when the deepest economic recession since the Great Depression stole the national spotlight. Advertising revenue for Tribune's newspapers had been shrinking dramatically for years, especially at the two flagship properties, the *Los Angeles Times* and *Chicago Tribune*, which ranked as America's fourth- and sixth-largest newspapers, respectively. Zell knew the bleeding was bad—he built a certain level of continued revenue deterioration into the deal—but he badly misjudged the severity of the continued decline and was about to fall off the pedestal he had put himself on many years earlier.

Ever the optimist, Zell saw the Tribune bankruptcy as being far from an unmitigated disaster. "True entrepreneurs never fail," said Zell. "Sometimes it doesn't work out, but they never fail."[2] From a financial perspective, he put "only" $315 million of his own skin in the deal. He was also a pioneer in a way, since Tribune's demise was followed less than four months later by the bankruptcy of crosstown rival Sun-Times Media Group. The skeptical media world saw it a bit differently. It had long since dismissed him as a foul-mouthed real estate cowboy out to wreak revenge on the journalists he so loathed. Chapter 11 was his ultimate comeuppance. Now he would be at the mercy of a bankruptcy judge. The king had most certainly lost his throne as well as his clothes.

Of far greater import to Zell was the potential damage to his personal reputation with financial institutions. He had spent decades cultivating partnerships and friendships that paid off when he needed them most, bailing him out of occasional mishaps. But the financial community was already in a state of turmoil. Tribune's demise was the latest chapter in a story of economic disaster that nearly derailed the world economy in late 2008, sweeping away the likes of Wall Street stalwarts Bear Stearns and Lehman Brothers. The entire American banking industry saw massive consolidation into a handful of behemoths like Bank of America, JPMorgan Chase, and Wells Fargo.

Regardless of the Tribune bankruptcy, Sam Zell has made himself a corporate presence impossible to ignore. Thanks to his contentious ownership of Tribune, "Zell Watch" is the ongoing pastime of professional journalists and media pundits alike, as he provides constant fodder for the endless stream of message boards, blogs, and other fields of chatter. Whether he likes it or not, his corporate movements will be more closely tracked than ever before—not because he pissed off most of the vigilant media but because his bravado and arrogance have made him a larger-than-life character.

In a quirky way, Zell's folly is likely to have a lasting impact on the future of media. As an unintended consequence of Tribune's bankruptcy, he brought needed attention and focus to the plight of global media companies as well as the future of the daily newspaper. Unfortunately, he was not able to turn around Tribune's flagging financial fortunes fast enough to beat the ticking debt clock. A collective sigh of relief could be heard in newsrooms across the country—finally, maybe, they would be rid of this four-letter distraction who cared little for their valuable role in society. But there was also the stark realization that Zell was merely the latest in a long line of would-be scapegoats. He was not the root cause of one of modern media's undeniable inevitabilities—the fact that the daily newspaper was dying.

Time will reveal the true significance of the Tribune's bankruptcy. In one way, shape, or form, it will rise from the ashes, either whole or as a trimmed-down version of its former self. Given Zell's own resilient nature, he likely will not skip a beat either. Only a month after the bankruptcy, he played the role of keynote speaker to another standing-room-only crowd at the University of California in Los Angeles.

Zell remains in hyperdrive, juggling his corporate responsibilities with an ongoing program to sniff out new investments on a global scale. He is the chairman of five New York Stock Exchange–listed companies—Equity Residential Properties Trust, one of the largest owners of apartments in the country; Equity Lifestyle Properties, an owner and developer of manufactured housing communities; Capital Trust, a real estate finance firm; Covanta Holding Corp., a leading waste-to-energy concern; and Anixter, a networking and cabling company.

His holdings in these companies give him billions to fall back on, though he saw his net worth—not to mention his *Forbes* ranking of number 205 on the list of the world's top billionaires—slashed in half from 2007 to 2008. His $3 billion kitty still puts him equal to the likes of Steven Spielberg and ahead of Giorgio Armani and Oprah Winfrey. Like many investors, his wealth got hammered by the tanking stock markets.

As Zell famously noted not long after purchasing Tribune, his large lifestyle would be left largely intact no matter how the deal shook out. He had no intention of slowing down, continuing to spend some 1,200 hours a year on his private jet (that's an average of three hours a day), combing the world for the next investment opportunity.

To be sure, Zell will continue to be a major force in shaping global trends in commercial real estate, where his legend remains largely intact and somewhat larger than life. "As any one single individual, he has had the greatest impact on the real estate industry," said Stanley Ross, chairman of the board of the University of Southern California's Lusk Center for Real Estate and a Zell contemporary with more than forty years in the business. "People in the industry want to know what his thinking is, and they look at it as they do their own strategic thinking. He is a visionary. It doesn't mean he's right every time, but he's a visionary."[3]

1

LITTLE BLUE PILL

"THE CHALLENGE IS, how do we get somebody 126 years old to get it up?" This was Sam Zell's unique way of saying hello to a large gathering at the *Los Angeles Times* shortly after taking charge of Tribune Co. in December 2007. "I'm your Viagra, OK? That's the name of the game, guys."[1]

It was a simple, yet jarringly unconventional opening line for a corporate executive to spring on an unsuspecting group of employees. But there it was. With one public reference to the "little blue pill," Zell made the first of what would become literally a torrent of cutting-edge statements during his tumultuous ownership of Tribune. Media world, meet Sam Zell.

Before he was announced as the winning bidder for Tribune, Zell was far from being a household name outside his native Chicago. After all, he was just another billionaire real estate investor, for the most part operating far beneath the gaze of the mainstream media in a deal-making, bricks-and-mortar world full of apartment buildings and towering office skyscrapers.

His most notable recent achievement had been a bit of incredible market timing and deal-making moxie only a few months earlier, when he cashed out of his beloved Equity Office Properties Trust for the princely sum of $39 billion. He personally pocketed a cool $1.1 billion to add to his enormous wealth, not a shabby payday after twenty years of building a company. He described the outcome in typical Zell fashion: "I think it was Confucius who said that 'money talks and bullshit walks.'"[2]

But it was Zell's remark at the L.A. *Times* that finally sat him on a national perch. And while it was quite an introduction, it was to be only the opening chapter in Zell's business playbook. Because his primary modus operandi was turning around distressed companies, he enjoyed initiating a personable, "meet the boss" program with every new acquisition. Zell used these early encounters to grandstand a bit and lay down the law, making clear that it was his money at risk and he would tolerate nothing less than a full commitment from the worker minions. He was ready to respect those who would return the favor and give him a chance.

In this case, his Viagra reference was a not-so-subtle hint. In fact, he was telegraphing his bold game plan for change. He was about to upset one of the oldest and most revered of old-school American media, and suddenly the entire world, at least the media world, cared. After all, here was a brash and largely unknown corporate intruder forcibly installed as the custodian of America's third-largest media conglomerate. That meant he wielded real power, potentially anyway. But who was he?

CLOAK OF CONFIDENCE

If first impressions are the only ones that count, then spying Sam Zell for the first time is not all that inspiring. He certainly does not look the part of a leading media mogul. Barely inching in at just over five feet tall, his most remarkable features are his large balding pate, closely cropped gray beard, and squinty eyes. For a sixty-something, though, he does keep his physique in remarkably trim fighting shape. This is not owed to any regimented workout routine, but rather a hyperactive nature and genetically gifted high metabolism.

When Zell opens his mouth, however, what you hear is what you get. There is no pretension. No bullshit. His gravelly, raspy voice and heavy Chicago accent command attention, completing his cloak of confidence and irascibility.

"Unique" is more than a buzzword when it comes to describing the present-day Sam Zell. It is a recurring theme. He is no technophile and refuses to use a BlackBerry. And yet how many billionaire CEOs have their own motorcycle gangs and ride bright yellow Ducatis to work? Underneath the leather jacket, Zell has a thing for sweaters and open-collared shirts. In fact, unlike many corporate chieftains, he rarely wears a suit. The dressed-down garb easily fits his persona as a self-made, go-against-the-grain contrarian. Practically speaking, however, Zell had a recurring skin condition dating back to his college days that made wearing anything tight around his neck nearly intolerable. When he recognized the marketing value of his dressed-down style, he kept it, adding jeans and loafers to the mix. And thus the image was complete.

Packed into Zell's casual yet diminutive physical frame is a highly complex character—straight-talking, hard-nosed and tough-minded, to be sure. Often he appears to have stepped directly out of some bygone era when corporate titans cared less about their public appearance or couth and more about making vast sums of money. He is an avowed Capitalist, a free-market thinker who despises Big Government and loves the art of doing deals. As he put it, "I just make money. That's what I do."[3]

Still, what does Zell do exactly that sets him apart from other entrepreneurs? He is asked that question, oh, about once a day. That may explain why Zell's favorite book is a tome titled *What Makes Sammy Run,* by Budd Schulberg, published in 1941, the same year Zell was born in Chicago. The book recounts the rags-to-riches-to-rags story of Sammy Glick, a charismatic Jewish boy born on the Lower East Side of New York, who early in life decides to escape the ghetto and climb the ladder of success, no matter who he has to clamber over on his way to the top.

Zell often refers to this book in personal conversations and in the dozens of speeches he gives every year at business conferences and educational forums. Aside from having a derivative of his name in the title, to Zell, the story mirrors his own life in many respects, in particular the struggles associated with winning, and sometimes losing, along the way.

"I am somebody who has been very fortunate to have had the opportunity to test my limits," said Zell. "And I would remind you philosophically that my definition of a fool is somebody who has reached his limits. Almost by definition, whatever goals you set, you need to constantly readjust them so that at no time do you reach your goals before your time is up."[4]

Standing atop a pulpit built from equal parts ego and bravado, Zell maintains a larger-than-life public persona that is constantly seeking new goals. But he is intensely guarded when it comes to keeping his personal affairs, well, personal. Family life is something Zell rarely discusses publicly. He prefers seeking publicity only for himself.

The immediate Zell clan includes his third wife, Helen; older sister, Leah; son, Matthew; and daughter Kellie from his first marriage and adopted daughter JoAnn from his second marriage. Of all the Zells, Leah is the one who has carved out her own business legacy. Together with her husband, Chicago businessman Ralph Wanger, she has run the Acorn International Fund, a mutual fund, for many years. Son Matthew is deeply ensconced in the family business as a managing director at Equity Group Investments, with his office just down the hall from his father.

It is a tight-knit group, to be sure, but also one that is prone to coming under the occasional microscope thanks to Sam's far-ranging and often very public exploits. When Leah started a new investment firm, Lizard Investors, in 2008, Zell was somewhat taken to task in the Chicago media for leasing her 7,500 square feet of space on the twenty-third floor of the Tribune Tower. The oak-paneled digs had a rich history, having once housed Tribune's executive offices, but had sat empty for months in the aftermath of Sam's takeover of the company.

To Zell, it was a clear-cut business decision and one that would still drive revenue to Tribune's bottom line. He cared little about the unintended publicity, but the move spoke volumes about his desire to push aside the status quo. The little blue pill was hard at work.

2

A "DIFFERENT" SORT

THOUGH BORN WITH an innate sense that he was somehow "different" from his peers, Sam Zell freely admits that his relationship with his father was a primary influence on the development of his complex character.

Only hours before the 1939 Nazi invasion that became the precursor to World War II, Zell's Jewish immigrant parents and older sister, Leah, fled their native western Poland. They had warned other family members of the impending conflict, but their pleas fell on deaf ears. "He was right then and he was never wrong again," said Zell.[1]

Over the better part of a year and a half, Berek Zielonka, his wife, Ruchla, and Leah made their way eastward across Russia. They often posed as tourists and lived off Berek's quick wits to avoid standing out in the crowd. They finally arrived in Tokyo, where they gained passage to the United States, traveling as many immigrants did at the time, aboard a cargo ship.

The Zielonkas landed in Seattle with little more than the clothes on their backs and $430 in Berek's pocket. Almost immediately, Berek decided to Americanize the family name, legally changing it from Zielonka to Zell. "Maybe Zell will ring the bell" he later joked about the new single-syllable moniker.[2] He also changed his first name to Bernard and Ruchla became Rochelle.

Back in his native Poland, Bernard had been a grain broker, and by all accounts a very successful one. Once in the States, he settled into the wholesale jewelry business, moving the family to Albany Park, Illinois, a community dominated by immigrant Jews just northwest of Chicago. There Sam was born on September 27, 1941.

The product of a strict and conservative religious family, Zell vividly remembered his father's influence on his young life. "I think the environment I grew up in, having the kind of father that I had, somehow or other dramatically impacted who I ended up being," recalled Zell. "There's this Yiddish word, *derechertz,* and it means respect. My father and mother, particularly my father, brought us up with the premise that respect was nonnegotiable. Love was optional. I'm not saying that in a bad way. It was, 'I want you to love me, but you have to respect me.' My dad was very, very strong, and very confident. I had to be very confident and strong to succeed in his shadow."[3]

TAKING PLAYBOY TO THE 'BURBS

As Sam was turning twelve, the Zell clan moved north to the tony confines of suburban Highland Park. Their new community lacked the proper facilities to continue young Sam's Jewish studies, so his parents sent him back into the city every afternoon on the Chicago North Shore Railroad to attend yeshiva, or Hebrew school. For Zell, the trip was akin to journeying to another world. Every afternoon, five days a week, he experienced a life that his Highland Park school chums could scarcely fathom. He made friends with the conductor. He befriended a group of much older girls from Wilmette High School. These encounters stuck with him, helping him feel at ease with women colleagues as he grew older. "I lived a kind of unique, separate life, because I went to school like everyone else, and then I got on the train," said Zell.[4]

Even at the tender age of twelve, it was no stretch of the imagination to see that Sam Zell had "entrepreneur" written all over his psyche. During his daily train rides into Chicago, Zell's inquisitive mind often worked in overdrive. One day in 1953, he was scanning the magazines on sale at the train station. There he found the first issue of a brand-new Chicago publication unlike any he had seen, or should have seen at his tender age. The magazine was aptly titled *Playboy* and founded by a little-known Chicago entrepreneur named Hugh Marston Hefner. At the time, *Playboy* was not the mainstream media product that it would become years later. In fact, it was considered so nefarious that its circulation was limited only to certain sections of the inner city.

Zell acted on his impulse, sensing an untapped commercial aspect to this exotic commodity. He bought *Playboy*s for fifty cents a copy and sold them to his suburban chums later in the day for three dollars. A salesman was born.

For many of today's most successful entrepreneurs, there is a seminal point in life, a time of discovery, if you will, when they get the equivalent of an epiphany, the eureka moment. Zell's came when he seized a golden opportunity to give a sermon on leadership and "taking chances" to his youth group. He was only twelve but he wowed the crowd with his powers of persuasion.

Zell found himself in the right place at the right time, able to marry his inborn salesmanship trait with the "you can make it in America" grounding derived from his immigrant roots.

His salesmanship served him well through his high school years, when he continued to display his entrepreneurial bent by selling photos taken at school events. He was also a standout student known for his unusually confident and forceful manner. The caption under his 1959 Highland Park High School yearbook photo says much about those formative years: "I'm not asking you, I'm telling you."[5]

COLLEGE LANDLORD

Early in his childhood, Zell learned the basic nuts and bolts of buying and selling real estate from his father, thanks to frequent dinner table banter and many a "father knows best" fireside moment. Zell described his father as a predictable, conservative investor, never overextending his reach, preferring safe plays to risky endeavors. At first, he was fascinated by the deal-making aspects of each transaction. But young Sam quickly became more interested in problem solving and finding solutions to prickly challenges. He developed a unique ability to quickly ascertain the hidden value of any investment by dissecting its fundamentals and measuring them against a supply-and-demand equation. This aptitude would be particularly important when it came to turning around distressed real estate that formed the early foundation of his would-be career.

When it came to a college education, Zell settled on the University of Michigan in Ann Arbor, a small college town. It was not too far from his native Chicago, yet distant enough to give him the independence he craved. There he majored in political science and received his BA and law degrees in 1963 and 1966, respectively.

During his senior year as an undergraduate, Zell decided to attend law school. He cared little for becoming a lawyer, but he felt that a formal legal education would be useful when it came time to do deals in his business career. He needed a place to stay for another two years, and by a stroke of happenstance, he stumbled into his first major real estate venture. When he heard that a developer was building a fifteen-unit apartment building on South Division Street near the University, he and a classmate pitched the idea of managing the property in exchange for free room and board. It worked. The developer then hired Zell to run another building around the corner, and soon he had more business than he could handle while attending school at the same time.

Zell had pledged to Alpha Epsilon, a large Jewish fraternity, and struck up a friendship with Robert Lurie. This quiet, thoughtful engineering student was quite the polar opposite to Zell's rambunctious persona, and yet the two clicked. Maybe it was their short statures, as together the two barely measured ten feet tall.

Lurie joined Zell in his fledgling apartment-management business, and Sam started looking for buildings to buy. With only $1,500 in savings, Zell parlayed the meager sum to purchase a land contract on a small apartment property. After a fresh coat of paint and some new furniture, he doubled the rents and went in search of more buildings to buy.

That's when local developer Don Chisholm gave him a huge break. Zell approached Chisholm to take over the management of his apartments across Ann Arbor. Again, his salesmanship worked. Chisholm was taken aback by Zell's brash, no-BS style and by his understanding of what his fellow students demanded. Soon Zell had grown his apartment management portfolio to some five thousand units.

By his last year in law school, Zell came face-to-face with his future. He had helped arrange the sale of a fellow law school friend's house near the University campus to Chisholm. Just as Chisholm was leaving for a stint in the Army Reserve, Zell decided to try his hand at assembling several houses on the same street so that a larger building could be developed on the site. The only problem was he lacked the funds needed to close on the property purchases.

Enter Zell's father, Bernard. After visiting Sam and Chisholm and listening to their plans, he was convinced to help them finance the deals. At that point, Sam seemed to have everything he wanted. But developing a project of the magnitude that Zell and Chisholm envisioned would take years. That meant a long-term commitment. To Zell, the prospect of graduating from law school and hanging around Ann Arbor was not so appealing. "I decided that I had to find out how good I was, and that I'd never be happy if I didn't really understand what I was capable of. I didn't think that I could really test that in Ann Arbor," he said.[6] His course would take him back home to Chicago. He sold off the apartment business to Lurie, graduated from law school, and headed west.

When Zell returned home, he learned another valuable lesson from his father—that geography and where properties were located had a big bearing on financial rewards. For example, his father's investments were generating a 4 percent return, while Zell's experience in Ann Arbor had delivered his investors 16 percent on their money.

Zell's first and only stab at full-time gainful employment came when he worked as an attorney at Chicago law firm Milberg Weiss. Surprisingly, he had few options. He could not figure out why he was having a hard time finding a job. Soon he had his answer. A senior partner at a major law firm pointed to Zell's deal-making history as the culprit. His entrepreneurial efforts signaled that Zell would not last three months as a lawyer, and no firm wanted to invest in training a short-timer.

That was a dead-on observation. But instead of three months, Zell lasted for all of one week before becoming bored with the whole legal profession. Once he learned he had to pay his dues, the jig was up and he took a chance on a brave tactic. He told the firm's senior partner he was going off on his own to do deals.

Remarkably, instead of unceremoniously tossing Zell out on his ear, the partner rewarded his bravado by agreeing to invest along-side him. One of Zell's first deals was the purchase of an apartment project in Toledo, Ohio. Over the next six years, he cast a wider net, acquiring apartment buildings in Madison, Wisconsin, in Lexington, Kentucky, and in Tampa, Orlando, and Jacksonville, Florida. All were secondary markets shunned by most major investors, but, ever the contrarian, Zell was happily pocketing big returns. Ultimately, Zell's experience in understanding the broad spectrum of investment options meant he would have little trouble raising money in the future.

By this point, Zell's business was taking off, but he yearned to spend more time selling and less time managing. He immediately thought of his old college colleague Lurie. The two easily reconnected, but little did they know that their business partnership would last the next twenty years. Together they formed Equity Finance and Management Co. in 1968. Using tax-advantaged investing tactics, along with some heavy borrowing thanks to Zell's salesmanship and close ties with several prominent lenders, they quickly developed into a major force in the real estate industry.

Ultimately their success was based on an unusual level of trust and compatibility, as well as a simple yet highly effective business strategy: buy distressed apartment properties, fix them up, and sell them for a healthy profit. While they were certainly not the only ones doing it, they leveraged their connections and track record to the hilt, making nonstop personal visits to the deep-pocketed sources of money—commercial banks, Wall Street investment banks, and institutional investors, including pension funds. The two also tested and discovered just how far they could push the envelope when it came to developing tax advantages to shelter their investments in the 1970s, at a time when the market was down and other investors were looking for the exits.

There was no question that both Zell and Lurie were driven to succeed. Years later, Zell recounted a humorous moment that embodied his philosophy during the era. "We were flying across the United States, and I said, 'Bob, come over to my seat.' I said, 'Here we are over Nebraska. Look down there. Do you realize how much real estate we don't own yet?'"[7]

3

GRAVE DANCER

FOR THE NEXT ten years, the odd yet tight-knit couple of Sam Zell and Bob Lurie snatched up distressed and bankrupt companies, riding out the ugly mid-1970s U.S. economic recession. They shunned the high-risk, high-debt development game, which saw many real estate titans, even the legendary Trammell Crow in Dallas, teeter on the brink of bankruptcy. In doing so, the duo garnered a national reputation for seeing trends that others could not. And Zell remained the front man for the business.

By 1978, editors at the Wharton School of Business's quarterly magazine, *Real Estate Review*, were certainly impressed with Zell's ability to harvest gold from the darkest despair—as well as the increasing depth of his pocketbook. He had donated $35 million to the university to start a new real estate management school, and they felt he was a worthy candidate to write a column for an upcoming issue. Rarely one to shirk an opportunity to tell everyone exactly how he feels, Zell agreed. It was the veritable win-win. His reputation would be cemented in one of the leading journals of the day, and he also was given the type of national platform he craved.

A respectable writer with a flair for blending matter-of-fact candor with a healthy dose of contrarian opinion, Zell thoughtfully penned his ode to the state of the markets. In a bit of sanguine fate, just before his deadline, he concocted the cryptic title "The Grave Dancer." It seemed only fitting, as he prominently boasted in his discourse that he often "danced on the skeletons of others." As the last line in the column noted, "You gotta' dance around the edge. But you don't fall in."

The headline became a moniker that would become forever synonymous with Zell, his mantra for the remaining chapters in his business life. And Sam approved. After all, Zell is a true believer in capitalism and the wealth of riches the system can bestow on those who take reasonable risks to achieve reasonable rewards. He is often characterized as a value investor, someone who sees value where others do not or cannot. Rolling up distressed businesses into newly frocked entities and then cashing out when market conditions are appropriate is his pragmatic, free-market approach.

Sensing the changing winds that would soon blow over the real estate industry, Zell and Lurie did something that left most of their investor peers scratching their heads. They closed the spigot on their property investments in the early 1980s. In 1981, they reaped some of what they had sown on their way to cashing out. For example, they sold Chicago's landmark Field Building for $94 million, making a hefty $42 million profit in just three years.

Zell described the real estate industry at the time as "a really shitty business," meaning that it had become crowded with investors looking to emulate his strategy. While imitation may be the sincerest form of flattery, Zell eschews copycats and competition.

As partners, as always, Zell and Lurie huddled for hours at a time, discussing the pros and cons of continuing with the new status quo they had set into motion years earlier. They had made millions on property over the past decade, but they wanted more. Ultimately they decided to turn their backs on real estate, for the time being at least. Instead, they would try their hand and test their business mettle in the corporate world. The idea was to diversify, to go outside their comfort zone, so as not to have all of their investment eggs in any one basket.

They carried no preconceived notions about how to buy and sell companies outside of real estate, but they viewed that as an asset rather than a liability. In particular, Zell believed that true entrepreneurs follow their instincts, based on what they see around them, and take a commonsense approach to the game of buying, running, and selling companies. Many in the real estate industry were envious of Zell's ability to shed his skin so easily. Most were mired, even trapped to a certain extent, in the only business they knew. They were willing to take chances on properties but not on their profession. Others secretly hoped that his outside-the-box forays would bring him crawling back to their bailiwick.

Together, Zell and Lurie started scanning newspaper headlines and talking to wider circles of bankers and other lenders in hopes of finding hidden treasures. They also set no hard-and-fast rules about what companies they would buy. Potential deals merely had to have the same basic characteristics—a company in a growth industry, in financial trouble or distress, which could be managed out of its doldrums into a potential market leader.

Using those criteria as their guide, the duo cobbled together a hodgepodge collection of companies, most having little to do with one another and absolutely nothing to do with real estate. Their goal was diversification, long before the term became just another cool buzzword in corporate lexicon, with half of their investments plowed into real estate and the other half into everything else.

One of their more interesting investments came in 1981, when

Zell and Lurie, along with businessmen Jerry Reinsdorf and Eddie Einhorn, took a stake in two local sports franchises, the Chicago White Sox baseball club and the Chicago Bulls basketball team. This bit of offbeat fun was largely Lurie's baby, for Zell had little patience or appreciation to play the role of spectator in any form of organized sports.

Zell's primary investment vehicle at the time was the Zell/Chilmark Fund, which he formed in 1985 with Chicago business associate David Schulte, whom Zell had come to know and trust over the years. With this fund, Zell adopted a longer-term strategy, telling investors they might not see significant returns for up to ten or twelve years. But Zell and Schulte traded on their names and reputations, attracting deep-pocketed pension-fund money from the likes of the State of Virginia Retirement System and Chicago's own Continental Bank.

Bottom fishing was the order of the day, as Zell/Chilmark invested primarily in bankrupt companies. Its first purchase was a shipping-container business called Itel Corporation, which had filed for bankruptcy in 1981. Little did Zell know that he would soon become the world's most renowned "shipping container maven." Under his management, by 1988, Itel was trading on the New York Stock Exchange and had quadrupled its annual revenues to $4 billion. The success came largely through both acquisitions and Zell's trademark approach to squeezing every last dollar out of the company's operations through tedious day-to-day management. He snatched up competitors and focused on reducing costs and redundancies—consolidating duplicate accounting teams, computer systems, etc.—to increase the company's value. When Zell sold off a division to General Electric in 1990, he pocketed a $250 million profit.

Other diversified investments ranged from the Delta Queen Steamboat Company to a 20 percent stake in fertilizer maker

Vigoro, which he sold in 1995 for $1.16 billion. He even owned Chicago-based Midway Airlines for a time. There seemed to be no rhyme or reason, no core theme at least, among the companies Zell purchased, other than the pursuit of profits. Synergies among his corporate properties were nonexistent, and he liked that just fine. He preferred to chalk up his success in the corporate world to simple blocking and tackling and conducting his own brand of independent research and soul searching before making a commitment.

By the late-1980s, however, distressed turnaround opportunities became scarce. But as one door was closing, a large and unlocked window was ready to open. Zell and Lurie were once again ready to hit the commercial real estate industry. With a vengeance.

NURTURED BY MOTHER MERRILL

Richard B. Saltzman, the head of real estate finance at Wall Street powerhouse Merrill Lynch, was the antithesis of the stereotypical wheeler-dealer—which is exactly why in many respects he was the perfect partner and foil for Zell. Like Lurie, Saltzman was smart with numbers and financing structures. With his thin wire-framed glasses, sandy hair, and bookish charm, he cut a preternatural low-key look, more like a professor than a high-powered investment banker. He was mild-mannered and unassuming and generally kept his business under the radar. And yet he used his position with one of America's largest financiers to good advantage.

At the time, 1988 to be exact, Merrill Lynch was the eight-hundred-pound gorilla on Wall Street. Under decades of strong and stable leadership, it dominated nearly every field of high-stakes finance—mergers and acquisitions, investment banking, personal finance, and public stock issuances. The firm became known to insiders as Mother Merrill for its nurturing of employees, cultivating talent, and eschewing layoffs even when profits were down. Merrill's ace in the hole in the late 1980s was its distribution network. Its access to consumers/investors through its stock brokerages made it the clear market leader.

Unlike many of his peers, who played a career game of musical chairs, bounding from one firm to the next in search of advancement—and the fattest bonus check—Saltzman felt right at home at Mother Merrill. He was a company man through and through, and he was amply rewarded for his loyalty, steadily rising through the ranks to eventually top out as chief operating officer of global investment banking in 2003.

Zell's chance encounter with Saltzman came in New York while he was attending a real estate conference. Saltzman recalled how he was impressed with Zell's quick and thorough analysis of the opportunity that existed for the right players—with money—in the market.

Together, they saw a train wreck in the making, just over the horizon, for commercial real estate. The late eighties and early nineties had produced an era of easy money, and that train was taking developers down the "build build build" tracks at a breakneck speed. Unfortunately, for that particular breed of risk takers anyway, it was about to jump the rails, and Zell and Saltzman wanted to be there to sweep up the mess with the largest pool of money they could muster.

READY FOR BOOM TIMES

Commercial real estate in the latter half of the 1980s was best characterized as the era of larger-than-life developers and brokers who became the talk of most major cities in America. Think "free-range chickens" roaming the countryside doing deals by day, while donning society garb to mix and mingle with corporate and civic power brokers by night. They were flush with money—though it belonged to other people most of the time—and everyone wanted to join in the deal-making orgy.

According to the Urban Land Institute in Washington, D.C., more office space was built across America's skylines in the 1980s than in the previous thirty years combined. Perhaps no American city better exemplified the go-go attitude of the mid-1980s better than Dallas, Texas. Every Thursday night was a real estate party. Tales of largesse abounded. Real estate entrepreneurs were using their newfound riches to open various night clubs, including the Tang-O and downtown's Stark Club (designed by a then-unknown architect named Philippe Starck).

But developers were mindlessly heading down a golden road that would turn to quicksand. For example, take CityPlace, an incredibly ambitious development proposing twin forty-two-story office buildings spanning Dallas's central arterial highway, Central Expressway. They would stand like two monolithic stone-clad goalposts against the Dallas skyline. Its jingly slogan spoke volumes about the overblown promise of the times—"The City with a Place for You."

The groundbreaking alone gave new meaning to the term "breaking ground." Just as nightfall descended on the city, a fleet of shiny black vans moved in unison, chauffeuring local real estate brokers and civic dignitaries alike deep into the bottom of a three-story pit. This cavernous hole in the ground would later become the first office tower's underground parking garage. For hours, patrons feasted on tasty Texas barbeque and wined and dined themselves well into Friday morning. But the late hour mattered not. These new titans did not work much on Fridays anyway.

The princely sum for the Texas-sized shindig? A cool $1 million, but that was just the tip of the marketing largesse. There was the limited edition embossed leather-bound brochure created especially for the occasion. The 150 exclusive copies were filled with computer-generated images of the gleaming stone and glass structures superimposed on images of the city's skyline by day and night. This was technology way ahead of its time for 1985, when a single computerized image cost an estimated $50,000 to reproduce.

Zell and Saltzman scanned the highbrow hubris unfolding before them and saw a confluence of warning signs that spelled trouble ahead. For true vulture investors, it had the makings of a new decade of opportunity. Those with cash to spend could swoop in to pick up distressed buildings at bargain prices. "We as an industry had committed hundreds of billions of dollars to unproductive usages," Zell observed. "And we had done so because the promise was 'build it today because it will cost more tomorrow,' not because there was any economic justification."[1]

THE PERFECT STORM

By 1989, Zell's reading of the tea leaves would turn out to be spot-on. The U.S. economy's spinning boom-and-bust dial was about to land in the bust zone again. A precipitous slide into a protracted recession would last through 1992 and the election of former Arkansas Governor William Jefferson Clinton as president. Just as President Ronald Reagan was saying his final farewells in the Oval Office in 1988, he was also closing an era known as the Reagan years, a period of seemingly boundless economic growth and prosperity. But that was all about to change.

The telltale signs were already there. Many called the confluence of events the perfect storm—interest rates were skyrocketing; free-lending bankers had fueled years of property overbuilding; and consumer spending was trickling to a standstill.

Certainly there is one generally infallible tenet when it comes to real estate developers—no matter how "disciplined" they might presume themselves, given access to easy money, they will feed at the trough and overindulge. They are, after all, human.

"If you go back and study all of the oversupplies, all are a result of excessive loan-to-value, thereby reducing the developer's risk," said Zell. "When you reduce the developer's risk, he becomes insensitive to building. If you don't have to put up real money—your money—and you don't have to take risk, then your ability to be an optimist is unlimited. It's an edifice complex."[2] This was one case in which the money talked, and the bullshit stubbornly refused to leave, like a bibulous guest overstaying his welcome at the party.

That million-dollar barbeque party back in Dallas, and many more just like it, were quickly generating a toxic by-product. Soon there would be a ten-year supply of freshly built office space in shiny glass-and-steel "see-through"—aka empty—skyscrapers all over Dallas. And Los Angeles. And Miami. And Chicago. You get the picture.

Banks and savings and loans were starting to feel the pinch of the staggering economy, which eventually led to the nation's first major mortgage meltdown. Many savings-and-loan executives were indicted and convicted of shady land dealings and extending overly generous credit to sketchy investors, especially on condominium projects and housing developments. The largest offender, Irvine, California–based Lincoln Savings & Loan Association, bilked investors out of billions and saw CEO Charles Keating imprisoned on charges of fraud and mishandling funds.

Wall Street, too, was in full retreat mode. New York Attorney General Rudolph Giuliani doggedly investigated the leading junk-bond firm, Drexel Burnham Lambert. Ultimately Drexel pleaded no contest to six felony charges—three counts of stock parking and three counts of stock manipulation—and paid a record $650 million fine. Then in December 1989, Drexel's top lieutenant, Michael Milken, the public face of the market, known as the junk-bond king, was fined $200 million and served two years in prison for a variety of securities-trading violations.

The image of Milken's ghostly mug on the cover of every major newspaper and magazine across the country was the final crack in Wall Street's facade. Layoffs became the order of the day, as more than thirty thousand once-powerful investment bankers suddenly found themselves without the means to support condos and houses on the Upper East Side and in the Hamptons.

The era was painfully portrayed in Tom Wolfe's novel *The Bonfire of the Vanities*, which excoriated the wretched excesses of Wall Street's overindulgent culture. In junk bonds, Wall Street had created yet another innovative financing mechanism, and once again old-fashioned greed had led to excesses.

As the schizophrenic decade was nearing its close, 1989 proved to be a big year for government intervention. On February 9, the U.S. government formed the Resolution Trust Corp., or RTC, to help financial institutions and property owners work through the inevitable foreclosures and asset sales. Under the auspices of the Federal Deposit Insurance Corporation, it was also there to restore some order and discipline after years of easy money and loose lending.

RAISING BILLIONS

Zell, too, had joined in a bit of the junk-bond hijinks, raising more than $1 billion, thanks in large part to Milken's help. But ultimately he remained deeply skeptical of the structure designed to heap enormous amounts of debt on companies while brokerage firms made short-term profits. He sensed the times were too frothy, so rather than wait for the impending bust, he unloaded assets even though it meant losses. He could never quite sign on to the long-term viability of junk bonds, viewing them as yet another example of Wall Street's unflinching addiction to short-term financial engineering.

Over the years, Zell has been accused of many things, but he adamantly defends his long-held belief in the long-term nature of real estate value. "I don't know anybody in the country who's a more long-term real estate investor than I am. I graduated from law school in 1966. I bought an apartment complex in Toledo, Ohio, in 1966 and paid off the mortgage in twenty-five years. I own it. There aren't very many people who can say that."[3]

Together Zell, Lurie, and Saltzman eschewed the junk-bond frenzy by creating two large "opportunity funds" in 1988 and 1989 that tapped the country's largest pension funds as primary investors. In other words, they were using other people's money, but people who could afford the admission price, were long-term investors, and were more accountable to their constituents.

Zell and Lurie's name cachet and promise of long-term mega-returns proved an immediate draw. The two funds raised more than $1 billion in only thirteen months—at the time considered an astounding achievement. And despite Zell's long-held belief that the lead dog in any pack has the best view, he recalled that it was actually lonely being in front of the crowd.

By now, it was also hard for Zell not to notice the declining health of his twenty-year business partner. Just when their little college-born venture was about to reach inconceivable heights of success, Lurie had developed colon cancer that would soon prove terminal. His untimely death in 1990 rocked Zell for a time. Only forty-eight years old, Lurie was survived by his wife, Ann, and six young children. Years later, Zell is still at a rare loss for words when trying to describe the relationship.

During Lurie's illness, Zell developed a habit of calling his partner every night, no matter where he was in the world, to catch up on business. After Lurie's death, he maintained the habit with Ann out of a sense of responsibility to the family Robert left behind.

Zell also eulogized his partner with major contributions to academic studies. In 1998, he permanently gifted the Wharton School at the University of Pennsylvania to found the Samuel Zell and Robert Lurie Real Estate Center. In 1999, Zell and Ann Lurie jointly donated $10 million to establish the Samuel Zell & Robert H. Lurie Institute for Entrepreneurial Studies at the University of Michigan's Ross Business School.

While the business world took notice of Lurie's passing, it inexorably moved on. One thing Wall Street abhors is a vacuum, and it wasn't long before others took notice of Zell's fund-raising success, spawning a bevy of imitators.

If Merrill Lynch was "Mother Merrill" on the Street, the stately matriarch of purebred financial power, then chief among her rivals was Goldman Sachs & Co., the new-monied interloper. Through its new private equity program known as Whitehall Funds, Goldman quickly invested more than $2 billion in pools of distressed RTC loans from 1991 to 1994 and either resold the properties or restructured the loans for a profit.

Goldman was not alone. The usual suspects—Lehman Brothers, First Boston, Apollo, the Blackstone Group, and George Soros—all created their own private equity funds to invest in problem properties. The vultures had turned to sharks, smelling blood in the water. Thanks to a fresh source of healthy capital, they were eagerly feasting on the dying assets that swashbuckling entrepreneurs had built as monuments to their own greed.

And they were racking up millions in the process as the economic recovery first began to take hold in 1992, just in time to start the roller-coaster boom-and-bust cycle all over again. In March, for example, Zell/Merrill Lynch Real Estate Opportunity Partners

L.P. II purchased the Bank One Center complex in downtown Indi-
anapolis from Citicorp for $115 million. And while Citicorp lost $30
million on the deal, Zell, ever the opportunist, positioned himself
to earn long-term fees by signing on to manage the property while
the markets found more solid footing. Between 1988, when Zell
launched the first opportunity funds with Merrill Lynch, and 2008,
private equity funds raised more than an estimated $100 billion to
invest in commercial real estate.

Meanwhile, Zell was still plowing money into a variety of corporate ventures. In only a five-month period from December 1992
to April 1993, the Zell/Chilmark fund invested in mattress maker
Sealy Corporation, the Schwinn Bicycle Company, and an oil and
gas concern called Santa Fe Resources. It also bought a significant
stake in the Revco drug store chain and took a 75 percent interest in
Carter Hawley Hale Stores, rescuing the retailer from the clutches
of bankruptcy.

Without Lurie's guidance, though, years of corporate financial
engineering finally caught up with Zell. On paper anyway, he was
worth a billion dollars. But as many investors learned the hard way
during the early 1990s, paper meant nothing without something to
back it up, namely cash in the bank to pay the bills. Just when those
bills were coming due, credit became a scarce commodity, and Zell
found himself in a market where it became impossible to refinance
his loans through the use of junk bonds.

Enormous debt bills were coming due, soon, and there wasn't
enough cash flow from his businesses to pay them. Zell's estimated
debt payments totaled $518 million in 1992, with another $539
million coming due in both 1993 and 1994. This period tested
even Zell's stubborn resolve. Plagued by many sleepless nights, he
watched his empire slowly withering under the weight of his debt
obligations.

But soon, Zell's past relationships bailed him out. Mother Merrill came riding to his rescue, loaning him enough cash to buy time to sell off selected assets to pay down some of his debt. He sold a 64 percent stake in his Manufactured Housing Communities Inc., which owned mobile-home parks in sixteen states. The plan was to package the stake as a mortgage-backed security to sell to the public. In other words, he was selling investors a piece of the debt pie. His lead underwriter on the deal? Merrill Lynch.

Therein lay another unique Zell trait—he quickly rebounds from his miscues, never losing sight of the next possible opportunity lurking just around the corner. This time around, an entirely new and complex industry had already caught his eye—broadcasting.

THE JACOR EXCURSION

One morning in 1993, while consuming his usual five newspapers over breakfast, Zell chanced upon a Cincinnati-based owner of radio stations called Jacor Communications. For months, Congress had shown a proclivity for easing regulations on the tightly controlled telecommunications industry. Though still mired in his debt issues, Zell decided to take a flyer on the company when he thought Congress would do even more, snapping up Jacor for the pittance of $50 million. As an opportunistic play, his timing was on the mark. Thanks to the U.S. Telecommunications Act of 1996, the broadcasting business was deregulated overnight.

Zell and Jacor CEO Randy Michaels cranked up the volume and went on a buying spree, growing the company from only 17 radio stations in 1996 to 234 by 1999, spending $2 billion over a single two-year period.

Zell then delivered on his promise to cash out at the peak of the market, selling Jacor to Clear Channel Communications for

$4.4 billion after it won a bidding war with CBS Radio. Zell's initial investment of $50 million turned into a $1.3 billion payday in only six years. That was an impressive return by any metric. It also helped cement Zell's national reputation as an astute countercyclical investor. He had become much more than a real estate mogul, although he never strayed far from his first true love.

BACK IN THE GAME

A renowned multitasker, Zell had also been keeping a keen eye on the commercial property markets. By 1993, he was already plotting his next moves as he quickly realized the game had changed. Debt, his least favorite four-letter word, was out. So he rolled with the punches and threw his entire organization into a radical 180-degree turn. Equity, aka going public via the stock markets, was in.

Zell had learned a valuable lesson in the previous cycle—the real estate markets were big, but they were one-dimensional and ponderously slow in reacting to change. Real estate is notoriously illiquid. It is all about tangible bricks-and-mortar physical stuff, and it is worth whatever the prevailing "market" says it is worth. Zell had bigger plans for the industry. He wanted to create a way to sell off pieces of buildings to individual investors by issuing stock. So once again, he turned to Wall Street for a few answers.

After spending the past decade amassing millions of square feet of space in apartments and office buildings, he discovered a unique investment structure created by the loathsome (to Zell anyway) U.S. government in 1960. Back then, Zell was still just a college freshman, but the real estate investment trust, or REIT, was about to make him one of the richest human beings on the good planet Earth.

On the road to REIT-land, the years that followed would see Zell involved in two of the most monumental events in commercial real estate history. The first was an epic, hard-fought takeover battle over the right to own New York's iconic Rockefeller Center. The second would see Zell cashing in on his status as REIT ringleader, selling off a huge chunk of his real estate empire in one whopper of a deal.

4

EDIFICE REX

AS ICONS GO, New York City's Rockefeller Center is among the grandest in America. And it would soon become the apple of Sam Zell's eye.

By 1995, Zell had carefully built a sky-high reputation for being the most astute real estate investor in the country. And yet he had not tackled a truly "marquee" or trophy building, a landmark that everyone recognized and could immediately associate with Zell's name. Like the lead character in the book *What Makes Sammy Run?* Zell was still striving to rise above his peers, to climb the next mountain, to test his limits.

With Rockefeller Center, he saw a golden opportunity to have his cake and eat it too. The grave dancer's sights became fixed on a high-profile victim of ill financial health in the financial capital of the world. If he could successfully negotiate a deal to buy the beloved icon, he would own one of the world's truly unique and one-of-a-kind properties. He would also forever carve his initials into the foundation of American business.

Zell found little not to like about Rockefeller Center. "When my daddy put me on his knee and taught me everything he knew about real estate, he told me location, location, location. And you don't find a much better location than Rockefeller Center, the heart of Manhattan, home of Radio City Music Hall, anywhere else in the world," he said.[1]

THE CENTER

Built and named after one of the country's wealthiest men, John D. Rockefeller Jr., Rockefeller Center is a symbol of urban renewal and entrepreneurial moxie, its limestone Art Deco motifs juxtaposed against the island of humanity otherwise known as Manhattan.

On any given weekday, the Center is home to sixty-five thousand workaday corporate soldiers, all navigating the daily scrum to arrive each morning at this central Midtown destination like so many ants to a magnificently sculpted mound. The Center also caters to scores of international tourists who come to visit the NBC store, see mega-productions at the venerable Radio City Music Hall, skate in the ice rink under the gaze of an imposing gilded statue of Prometheus, or just plain gawk at the grandeur of the place.

Rockefeller Center Properties Inc., or RCPI, a real estate investment trust, owned the Center in partnership with the Rockefeller family trusts that Junior had established in 1934. But unlike so many of Manhattan's towering properties, Rockefeller Center has a short list of owners in its illustrious history. And that is precisely what makes it one of the most highly valued and prized possessions for any true-blue property mogul.

When Rockefeller Center opened in 1939, it brought to life more than 6 million square feet of office and retail space in twelve buildings, spanning a swath of New York City from fashionable Fifth

Avenue on the east over to Seventh Avenue and from West Forty-first Street up to West Forty-eighth Street. It also became the epitome of new Corporate America.

Decades later, however, Rockefeller's dream became the family's nightmare. Some fifty years after its completion, almost to the day, the Center would face its greatest challenge for financial survival.

THE SLIPPERY SLOPE

By 1995, Rockefeller Center had fallen on hard times. First the deep recession of the early 1990s struck the nation's office markets with a vengeance. The deadly combination of huge job losses and a building boom at just the wrong moment packed a double whammy for owners of office buildings.

While Rockefeller Center had been largely immune to such economic gyrations over the decades, a series of financial miscues put it on the brink of collapse. The untimely sale to Japan's Mitsubishi Estate Company in 1989 and rents predicated on $65.00 a square foot (they were actually averaging half that for most of the 1990s) spelled trouble ahead. In 1992, gross revenues for the twelve buildings in the trust were $229 million versus the projected $312 million it needed just to break even. More bad news—in 1993, the Center was appraised at only $1.2 billion, or $400 million less than a year earlier.

At the same time, costs were skyrocketing. The Center was in the midst of a massive $300 million maintenance program designed to modernize its operating systems. The move was needed both to maintain its existing tenant roster and to attract potential new tenants.

In a last-ditch effort to stave off a bankruptcy that would have embarrassed the good Rockefeller name, David Rockefeller jetted to Tokyo to meet with Mitsubishi Estate's new president, Takeshi Fukuzawa. He carried in his briefcase a new plan that would rescue the property thanks to a $60 million injection of fresh cash. But the trip was doomed from the start, in many ways mirroring the folly of the entire Rockefeller Center fiasco. First, Rockefeller's car dropped him at the wrong building. In his haste to be on time, in the middle of a driving rain, he slipped and fell on the cold, soaked street in front of Mitsubishi's headquarters, breaking his leg in four places. Still, in excruciating pain, he carried on with his presentation from a wheelchair.

In the end, Rockefeller's trip did little to sway the tough-minded Mitsubishi executives. On May 11, 1995, the company forced Rockefeller Center into Chapter 11 bankruptcy protection after it failed to come up with enough cash to meet the payments on the Center's burdensome $1.3 billion mortgage.

ONE ZELL OF A TIME

By now, this bit of corporate drama was becoming the prime hunting ground for one Sam Zell. Long before he saw the first Chapter 11 headlines in his hometown *Chicago Tribune* newspaper, he had already surmised that Rockefeller Center's predicament spelled opportunity. And his timing was razor sharp.

Sensing that RCPI could be convinced to foreclose on Mitsubishi and take control of the Center if presented with an attractive offer, Zell quickly assembled a group of blue-chip investors, led by the Walt Disney Company and General Electric. He chose his partners carefully, knowing that each would have a vested interest in owning this prime real estate. Disney was primarily interested in the Center's retail and entertainment venues, including Radio City Music Hall. Meanwhile GE, owner of the NBC television network, was one of the Center's primary tenants and had an obvious stake in the outcome of the battle over its corporate home.

Never one to dawdle, Zell struck fast with his troika, with an initial agreement to invest $5.00 a share, or the equivalent of $250 million, to buy a 50 percent interest in Rockefeller Center Properties in mid-August 1995. From the get-go, the offer was warmly received. "This will result in a new entity with a much stronger capital structure with far less debt," wrote Stephanie Leggett-Young, the real estate trust's corporate secretary and spokeswoman. "Shareholders would benefit from having an owner-operator with the expertise that Sam Zell could bring to this."[2] Under his terms, Zell and the Zell/Merrill Lynch Real Estate Opportunity Partners Limited Partnership III would own most of the Zell group's stake.

The move sent shudders through the real estate industry. At first, many believed that Zell had finally fallen victim to his own version of an "edifice complex," an all-too-common investment mistake and a trap he had for years vehemently warned others to avoid. Zell insisted otherwise. "I don't invest in anything other than economic prospects," he bristled. "If it's not economic, I'm not interested." It's not that he doesn't appreciate the finer things in life or their place in history. He just stubbornly refuses to be swept away by emotions that could cloud his own vision of what constitutes value investing. That would be so "uncontrarian."

Not long after Zell's initial salvo was delivered, however, the early signs pointed to a protracted and difficult path to a final deal. Mitsubishi was one stumbling block, as it was intent on holding on to its billion-dollar baby. It held most of the aces in this hand, at least until September 12, when it was required to file a plan of reorganization to emerge from four months of Chapter 11 bankruptcy protection.

Complicating matters, another well-heeled suitor was already waiting quietly in the wings. Goldman Sachs and the Whitehall

Street Real Estate Limited Partnership V (an affiliate of Goldman and New York's Tishman Properties) had already bailed out RCPI just nine months earlier with a $225 million cash lifeline, postponing bankruptcy. In the process, Goldman became the Center's largest creditor and naturally wanted a voice in the proceedings.

The group also had cleverly negotiated a right to reject any takeover bid for the REIT, and had the right to purchase up to 20 percent of the company at only $5.00 a share. This entrenched position would become the primary sticking point in thwarting rival bidders' plans. Asked if he foresaw obstacles to his bid to control one of the world's landmark properties, Zell replied with a blunt dose of realism, "Lots."[3]

In the midst of one of the biggest deals of his career, Zell continued to display a remarkable capacity for multitasking—a billion-dollar deal here, another one there. The same week he bid on Rockefeller Center, Zell convinced another New York institution, Federated Department Stores, to buy out his 54 percent ownership stake in Broadway Stores. Zell had rescued the retail chain from bankruptcy, but even years later, he was having some difficulty in turning it around financially. Federated, however, was on a buying spree, having purchased R. H. Macy four months earlier for $4 billion. It paid a cool $1 billion for Broadway, or double its stock market value. The deal surprised nearly all of Wall Street's oddsmakers, who were betting against the grave dancer's ability to turn that particular ugly duckling into a swan.

With the Broadway sale put to bed, Zell threw all of his attention into the Rockefeller Center transaction. His legal training helped him to better understand the complexity of deal structures like the convoluted labyrinth of trusts and partnerships that were the hallmarks of the Rockefeller ownership equation. "Rock Center is interesting because it has an unending number of players, both real and potential," said Zell. "It's like a jigsaw puzzle with an enormous number of moving parts, and the person who can see them all and know why they're moving and where they're moving will win."[4]

Ultimately, he viewed the entire exercise as a personal test of his problem-solving skills, of which he had many. Plus, when push came to shove, he loved a good fight. But he also knew from the get-go that he would only go so far, take only so much risk, before he would push away from the bidding table.

A real estate man at heart, one of Zell's trademarks is "walking the property" to see firsthand not only the obvious physical components, but also the innate synergies that might exist throughout the mini-city. During his due diligence of the deal, which included an hours-long inspection of every square inch of the Center, Zell found hidden gold where Mitsubishi had not. The Rockefellers certainly kept their gem polished, spending more than $500 million on upkeep and maintenance since Mitsubishi's partnership began in 1989. Though costly, the attention to detail was obvious—a fifty-year-old property that shone brighter than a freshly cut diamond.

Opportunities to grow revenue were already surfacing. GE had floated its interest in buying its own building, known as 30 Rock, for its signature headquarters. And on paper anyway, the huge retail space, 500,000 square feet of it, half the size of a traditional mall, looked to be among the most valuable in the city, given the high volume of pedestrian traffic. Zell's experience across a broad spectrum of real estate types, including retailing, came into play. He could see upside here by replacing the hodgepodge of souvenir shops and lesser-known restaurants with higher-paying tenants.

Whether other bidders saw the same value proposition as Zell is still unclear. But they certainly saw competing sharks in the water and quickly swam into the deep end, attracted by the notion of winning a bidding war.

THE BATTLE COMMENCETH

Twenty-four hours is an eternity on Wall Street when it comes to starting a battle royal.

The day after RCPI's board accepted the Zell group's bid, noted New York real estate investor Tishman Speyer Properties launched its own play for the property. Representing an investor group that included the Lester Crown family of Chicago, Tishman president Jerry Speyer's bid proposed buying "a substantial stake" in one of the partnerships that owned Rockefeller Center as well as purchasing the Center's mortgage from RCPI for $975 million and giving the trust's shareholders a 21 percent stake in a new company that would hold the mortgage.

Zell fancied himself as equal parts caretaker and custodian of the complex, referring to other bidders as "slicers and dicers" who were only interested in selling off pieces of the Rock to the highest bidders. But that characterization of Speyer, a native New Yorker known for his reputation as a long-term property holder and mega–civic booster, was well off the mark.

In a follow-on volley, Zell then put his money where his mouth was, loaning RCPI $10 million after it had to fork over all of its revenue in a $33 million payment to Goldman at the end of August. As the September bankruptcy hearing approached, Zell was in full courtship mode, laying on the charm with RCPI's top brass. "I'm known as a tough guy and maybe I am, but I've learned it's a lot more fun to make love than to make war," he remarked.[5]

Zell's overtures worked, as RCPI's board rejected the Tishman bid as inadequate. But the specter of two simultaneous deals attracted attention from other suitors. Soon several new investor groups, including Leucadia National Corporation, Gotham Partners L.P., Goodman & Company Ltd., a Canadian asset management firm, and Oak Hill Partners, a Los Angeles real estate firm, began stirring the pot from inside the company.

Each owned an interest in RCPI, and as a voting block threatened to veto the deal already struck with Zell. Instead, they wanted RCPI to pursue a "shareholder rights offering." Under that scenario, shareholders could buy rights to purchase issues of future shares on a pro rata basis, and large shareholders would pledge to purchase any rights that were available if smaller shareholders chose not to buy into the offering. The groups estimated that the rights offering could raise at least $105 million, which could then be combined with a senior loan of around $350 million to replace some of the trust's high-cost debt and give it the financial wherewithal to operate the property.

But many observers, including Zell, believed the investor groups were merely jockeying to extract a better offer from him, a tactic with which Zell was intimately familiar. After all, at the time Zell struck his deal, RCPI stock was trading at around $8.00 a share, and the company's forty thousand shareholders, half of whom were individual investors, had seen the stock price gyrate wildly over the years, from a high of $22.00 to as little as $4.25.

Then on October 1, a surprising letter was delivered to the RCPI offices. Seemingly out of the blue, family patriarch David Rockefeller rekindled the earlier bid of Goldman Sachs and Tishman, offering to buy the REIT for $295.5 million, or $7.75 a share in cash.

The heat to buy this slice of prime Manhattan real estate had been cranked up a notch, and Zell was feeling it. Nearly four weeks later, in a letter to RCPI chairman Peter Linneman (who years later became head of Zell's international investment group and a Wharton School of Business professor), Zell made one last run at the company. Under his new plan, shareholders would receive between $7.49 and nearly $9.00 a share if the board could negotiate away its loan agreement with Goldman Sachs.

Zell cleverly sought to rid the deal of what he considered its greatest impediment, Goldman and Whitehall Street. He offered to repay the $191 million that the REIT owed them and pay Whitehall $30 million for the warrants it held to buy up to 19.9 percent of the REIT. Ever the salesman, Zell pointed to his own calculations, saying his new bid would give Whitehall at least a 50 percent return on its loan to the REIT. "Given that Whitehall is typically not a long-term investor, we assume the Whitehall investors would find this proposal very attractive," Zell wrote Linneman.[6]

But by this time, the RCPI board seemed swayed by Goldman's bid and Zell's offer appeared too little, too late. After several weeks of waiting, Zell became impatient, and formally withdrew his amended offer, paving the way for a final resolution. The bidding had gotten too rich for Zell's risk/reward tolerance. He had offered his best and final, and he no longer cared if others were willing to up the ante. He was folding his cards.

In July 1996, nearly a full year after the initial deal with Zell, Rockefeller Center Properties was sold to the Goldman Sachs/Tishman Speyer/Rockefeller group. In an interesting twist, Mitsubishi and the Rockefeller family trusts retained a minuscule stake in the property to avoid significant tax liabilities, a tactical trademark often employed by Zell. Finally, Rockefeller Center was back in the hands of a Rockefeller.

Zell's partner, Disney, walked away with nothing, while GE's NBC unit purchased the 1.6 million square feet of space it occupied in 30 Rockefeller Plaza for $40 million in April 1996.

For his part, Zell was left a bit battered but certainly not bruised. He did pocket an $11.5 million "breakup" fee as part of a provision in his original contract in case RCPI found another buyer. More important, he leveraged his role in the high-profile deal-making to his advantage. His name had topped the business headlines in the *Wall Street Journal* and the *New York Times* for months. Plus, he had shown a certain amount of discipline in not being blinded by Rockefeller Center's luster. He pulled out when the bidding became too rich, a feat that is more than most real estate moguls could match.

Years later, Linneman reflected on the tense negotiations with Zell. "It was a very complex time and a very complex situation, but I always found negotiating with Sam and dealing with Sam as very easy. I tend to be very straightforward. I know what is important to me and I'm very clear about stating it and if I don't understand something I state what I don't understand. And he's the same way. It wasn't easy, but it was very straightforward."[7]

5

EQUITABLE ARRANGEMENTS

WITH THE ROCKEFELLER Center dust-up fading in the rear-view mirror, Zell continued on his somewhat zealous course of real estate empire building. Though the titanic battle for New York's crown jewel grabbed the majority of national headlines, Zell is a deal-making dervish, constantly in the throes of several major transactions at any one time. He is always on the hunt for new challenges. Such was the case in 1996, as he prepared to go public with his largest real estate venture to date, one that would see him single-handedly change the face of one of America's largest remaining empires, the $6.5 trillion commercial real estate industry.

By now, Zell had long since ingrained the moniker "equity" in many of his companies—Equity Office, Equity Residential, Equity International. To Zell, the term has several connotations, not the least of which is his driven need to accentuate the positive "ownership" aspect when it comes to investing. In real estate parlance, the term "return on equity" also has profound significance as one of the ultimate measures of success. It is viewed as both the value received from investing one's own money in a deal as well as the increased value of a property—minus the mortgage debt—that would be realized upon a sale.

Zell's investment ethos is grounded in making money by pumping equity into companies, preferably those in dire straits, just when they need it most. Time and again, he has demonstrated that when there was demand for rescue capital, he was there to supply it. However, that does not mean he is free-spending or capricious with his dough. Zell is no cheapskate, but he does believe in putting as little of his own skin, or equity, in the game as possible in hopes of winning the big prize. He measures and supplies exactly what is needed, no more and no less. And if along the way he pays Uncle Sam as little in taxes as legally possible, so much the better.

By mid-1996, Zell was looking for just the right investment vehicle in which to roll up his first two successful Zell/Merrill Lynch funds. That's when he was introduced to the real estate investment trust, or REIT, which had become a hot property. Created by law back in 1959 thanks to President Dwight D. Eisenhower, REITs are structured to pay out at least 95 percent of their annual income to shareholders. In return they are exempt from federal taxes. They appeared to fit Zell's tax-averse profile to a tee.

His pal at Merrill Lynch, Richard Saltzman, had helped take New Jersey shopping center owner Kimco Realty Corporation public in 1991 to much fanfare. Given that Zell is an exploiter of opportunity, and the small fact that he was sitting on billions of dollars worth of commercial real estate he had acquired over the past decade, that was the green light Zell was looking for. He was ready to hit the REIT road.

MOBILE-HOME MAVEN

As far back as the mid-1980s, Zell and his partner Robert Lurie had started Mobile Home Communities Inc. (MHC), which owned and operated forty-one manufactured-housing communities, mainly in fast-growing Sun Belt cities. Their love of rental units came during their formative years as college landlords, but Zell recognized the growth potential of this decidedly unglamorous but low-cost alternative to site-built single-family housing.

Zell was also way ahead of his peers in grasping the implications of the "graying of America." Ever fascinated by demographic trends, he often focused on population movements and aging profiles to figure out his next investing moves. In the midst of his digging, he found that the mobile-home industry was highly fragmented, with lots of individual, independent, and local owners of mobile-home parks scattered around the country, so-called mom-and-pop operators.

Certainly crunching the numbers made sense. It cost only $23 per square foot of space to buy a mobile home versus more than $50 per square foot for a site-built home. The homes were literally manufactured in a factory and then driven by roadway to the home site. Construction costs and time were measured in days instead of months for more traditional single-family homes. This business had low-cost, high-return efficiencies written all over it.

Seniors and retirees, in particular, were Zell's primary target. As a result of their community feel and low prices, mobile-home parks made perfect sense for those on fixed incomes who still longed for the American dream of home ownership.

Zell quickly surmised that the industry could be consolidated and commoditized with the right capital backing. So he changed the company's name to Manufactured Home Communities—it sounded a bit more professional—and took it public as a REIT in March 1993, raising nearly $200 million. Straight out of the gate, MHC was the king of the mobile-home world, with fifty communities in seventeen states and more than sixteen thousand homes. Shortly after the initial public offering, Zell bought up four thousand more home sites, and in 1994 the company took off, ending the year with sixty-seven communities and twenty-five thousand home sites.

Zell's ability to create public companies gave him a unique advantage when it came to raising money for acquisitions, which were funded by new share offerings and a two-for-one stock split. In 1994, 80 percent of MHC residents were retirees, while 20 percent were young adults. But soon, the low cost of owning a home in one of Zell's communities began making sense to younger Americans as well.

Zell continued acquiring some of the best mobile-home parks in the country, often located near top resorts and vacation spots that were a natural magnet for attracting retirees. In another trademark Zell move, he also focused on aggressive internal cost controls, which reduced administrative expenses to less than 10 percent of total revenues. Yet again, he was creating a low-cost industry leader.

When Zell senses he can totally dominate an industry, he takes the bit between his teeth and makes a run for it. "Unless you're the lead dog, the scenery never changes," he noted. In 1996, Zell made his most aggressive bid to grow MHC by offering $400 million to acquire Chateau Properties Inc., a Michigan-based REIT with forty-seven communities and over twenty thousand sites. Zell's offer was unsolicited and was quickly put together in response to an announced merger between Chateau and Colorado-based ROC Communities Inc. That "merger of equals" through a stock swap would have created serious competition to Zell and his plans to dominate and consolidate the industry. In other words, he was willing to interject himself between Chateau and ROC to avoid the competition.

Much to Zell's chagrin, after months of protracted negotiations and back-and-forth offers and counteroffers, the Chateau and ROC boards approved their merger in February 1997. The combined entity usurped Zell's MHC as the largest owner of manufactured-housing communities in the United States.

To say that Zell was an unhappy camper would be a gross under-statement. He would never be described as a gracious loser. His competitive nature does not allow for glad-handing or finishing in second place. "Second is the first loser," said Zell. To him, nothing but winning really counted, and he has been known to stubbornly pursue an object of his desire until he gets what he wants.

True to his nature, six years later, Zell made yet another run at Chateau, but was outbid by Chicago-based private firm Hometown America, which purchased Chateau for $2.2 billion with back-ing from the Washington State Investment Board. Apparently Zell was a good teacher—the head of Hometown America was Barry McCabe, a former MHC president who left in 1995 to start his own company with two of Zell's former money-raising colleagues.

By 2004, based on his own analysis of the manufactured-housing market, Zell sensed a new opportunity to grow the business organi-cally rather than by acquisition. He believed that the industry was ready for rather dramatic changes, including a broader appeal to middle-aged and more-affluent Americans who were hitting the road in their recreational vehicles in an attempt to re-create the expe-riences of their youth in rediscovering America. Many of MHC's properties had unused acreage that would be prime areas for the growing crop of RVs.

First came a much-needed rebranding exercise, replacing the perfunctory Manufactured Housing Communities name with one of his tried-and-true "equity" monikers. Overnight, MHC became Equity Lifestyle Properties, traded on the New York Stock Exchange under the new symbol ELS. Over the next four years, Zell snapped up several smaller companies and readied ELS to exploit the new growth era.

By 2008, ELS boasted a market value of $1 billion and owned more than three hundred communities with 112,000 sites in twenty-eight states and British Columbia. In a bold move, Zell named Joe McAdams as ELS's new president in January 2008. McAdams, a former ELS board director, had founded Privileged Access, a recreational-vehicle and vacation-membership business. As president, he was tasked with creating new marketing programs geared to the RV and outdoor enthusiast crowd, including RVonthego Club, a loyalty-based membership club.

"In 2007, the view of home ownership began a sea change," said Zell. "While it remains part of the American dream, it is now being coupled with a desire for reduced real estate costs, capital preservation and financial security. A three-bedroom, two-bath home that averages about $80,000 in our amenity-packed resort communities in Arizona, Florida or California is the new paradigm that we think will appeal to the 25 percent of Americans who are either part of the Baby Boom generation, empty-nesters or already retired. The quest is for high quality, but low cost alternatives in desirable retirement and vacation locations, where they are surrounded by family and friends. The movement is toward communities of like-minded people that stress a lifestyle based on social interactions and friendships. The generation that worked hard and accumulated wealth is now ready to turn that same energy into filling their lives with meaningful personal connections and a strong social fabric, without financial strain."[1]

APARTMENT KING

Thanks to the Zell/Merrill Lynch funds of the 1980s, Zell was flush with thousands of apartment properties he had acquired, often from distressed owners who were overextended on their loans. He and Barry Sternlicht, then working with the wealthy Ziff and Burden families in New York, cobbled together their apartment assets to form Equity Residential Properties Trust (EQR) in August 1993. (Sternlicht would later found Starwood Hotels Corp., one of the largest hotel firms in the world.)

To Zell's delight, EQR began life in the enviable position as the nation's largest apartment landlord, with twenty-two thousand apartment units in thirty cities. To lead his apartment operation, Zell tapped into his unique ability to spot leaders when he named Douglas Crocker, a veteran apartment manager and Harvard graduate, as CEO. Zell liked to surround himself with innovators, and Crocker had new ideas coursing through his veins.

Crocker's plan mirrored Zell's own innovative thinking. He devised a simple supply/demand formula—target growth cities where new development would be difficult, those with tough zoning laws which could help prevent competing apartment developers from building. He also brought a new level of professionalism to the apartment industry, thanks to the creation of a bulk buying program to cut costs and the formation of "Equity University" to formally train all of EQR's property managers under a uniform set of operating principles.

Fully engaged in the business, by 1995 Zell relied on his market timing. Sensing that property prices had bottomed, EQR went on a shopping binge. As one of the largest of the publicly traded apartment owners, over the next two years EQR used its access to substantial capital to gobble up Wellsford Residential Property Trust for $620 million and Evan Withycomb Residential Inc. for $625 million in 1997.

When shares of REITs were slumping in 1998, and as smaller players were looking for the exits, market-leading EQR still had its capital and Zell was still buying and in larger chunks. He picked up Merry Land & Investment Co., a major apartment owner in the Southeast, for $1.54 billion in stock and the assumption of $656 million in debt, adding nearly 35,000 apartment units in nine states. A year later Zell paid $730 million for Lexford Residential Trust and its 36,000 units in 16 states.

Unlike many traditional real estate moguls, Zell also knows when it is time to cut his losses and run. In the economic slowdown of the post-9/11 era, EQR adjusted to the new realities of lower apartment rents and higher home ownership trends. It sold off unprofitable communities and slashed rents. The company did such a good job under Crocker's steady hand at the day-to-day management wheel that it landed a coveted spot on the S&P 500 stock index.

Even as Crocker retired in 2004, ushering in a new management team, ever-shifting demographic trends once again put Zell in the right place at the right time. Just as the U.S. home ownership rate peaked at 69 percent in 2004, Zell had strategically placed the company directly in the path of the next wave of apartment renters, the children of the Baby Boom generation known as Echo Boomers. By 2008, EQR had realized Zell's dream of building the largest owner of apartments in the United States, with 554 properties and nearly 150,000 apartments. From this leadership position, the company became a bellwether for the entire industry. And Sam was pleased.

BUILDING AN OFFICE BEHEMOTH

Mobile homes and apartments are interesting enough, but the true icons of commercial real estate are those steel-and-glass behemoths known as office buildings. To gauge the strength of this iconic asset class, consider that the value of the U.S. office building market is larger than the gross domestic product of Spain.

Here again, thanks to his formation of the Zell/Merrill Lynch funds in the 1980s, Zell had already accumulated enough office real estate to form the largest office REIT in the world. A prescient market timer throughout his career, Zell once again was in the right place at the right time. In the mid-1990s, the U.S. economy was positively booming and Corporate America was expanding at a rapid rate into the type of marquee office towers that Zell owned. To a certain extent, it could be argued that luck played a crucial role here, but Zell would argue that he put himself squarely in the path of opportunity.

GOING PUBLIC

With the groundwork laid, Zell was ready to take his Equity Office Properties Trust public. On that fateful day, July 8, 1997, EOP offered 25 million shares at $21 each on the New York Stock Exchange. After its first full day of trading, the stock closed at $26.875 after 12.5 million shares were traded. Several days later, the stock offering was sold out, including 3.75 million over-allotment shares from the offering's underwriters, Wall Street powerhouses Merrill Lynch (as lead underwriter), Lehman Brothers, Morgan Stanley, Prudential Securities, and Smith Barney.

By then, EOP was the largest office REIT in the world, operating ninety office properties with 32.2 million square feet in twenty states and the District of Columbia, as well as fourteen stand-alone parking facilities. But that was not nearly enough for Zell. He had the cash and he was spending.

Only weeks after the ink was dry on the IPO, several deals would augment EOP's standing as the driving force in the industry. In September 1997, EOP acquired its largest competitor, Boston's Beacon Properties Corporation, for $4.3 billion. By then, EOP shares had gained more than 50 percent in value, and the Beacon purchase increased EOP's size by 51 percent.

Once again, Zell was delivering on his "bigger is better" mantra to his investors. In announcing the Beacon deal, Zell told analysts on a conference call, "We view ourselves as the dominant player in a gigantic industry. Our scale will separate us from everyone else."[2] Clearly Zell wanted to be the lead dog in the fight for market supremacy. It also mattered that the value of his own stake in EOP was multiplying with each new investment. His burgeoning wealth was quickly separating him from the rest of Chicago's business elite.

Through the rest of the 1990s, Zell put EOP's financial muscle to work, strong-arming his way through an acquisition binge and buying up anything that wasn't literally nailed down. In 1998, he snapped up twenty-eight buildings for $2.4 billion. Ever the innovator and risk taker, Zell also launched EOP Access, a division dedicated to driving more revenue through the sale of business services to tenants, including telecommunications.

In 1999, EOP acquired another 1.9 million square feet of property for $400 million. In February 2000, it ratcheted up the deal making, swallowing New York–based Cornerstone Properties with its eighty-six buildings in a $4.6 billion gulp. With each new purchase, he was quickly infilling major markets in which EOP lacked a significant, or dominant, presence. He also was in control of the world's largest real estate company. In only three years since going public, EOP had tripled in size, with 380 office buildings totaling a mammoth 95.5 million square feet. And with Zell, dominance truly is king. "If you're the biggest kid on the block, you can throw your weight around. Of course, I never was the big kid, but I've made up for it over the years."[3]

After only a three-year hiatus, Zell would once again have a shot at being the big kid to buy Rockefeller Center, after Goldman Sachs put it up for sale yet again in 1999. And once again he would square off against Jerry Speyer. This time around, a whole new cast of real estate moguls would bid on the Center, including Mortimer

Zuckerman, head of New York's Boston Properties, Steve Roth, head of Vornado Realty Trust, and the wealthy Crown and Fisher families from Chicago and New York, respectively.

Ultimately, though, in late 2000, Speyer would again win the day, seizing complete control of Rockefeller Center in a deal valued at $1.85 billion and spelling an end to the Rockefeller family's involvement in what was one of the true golden ages of real estate. Though he had the financial muscle to pull off any price for the Center, Zell bowed out when the bidding level began making less sense to him.

Zell was somewhat comforted by the knowledge that with or without Rockefeller Center in his portfolio, he had transformed the very nature of the public real estate markets. "Taking the U.S. commercial real estate business beginning in 1992, along with a number of other people in the industry, and turning it into a $350 billion industry, liquid real estate, something that had never been done before, is not only something I'm proud of but is a reflection of recognizing an opportunity and adjusting what you do to reflect the opportunity that's given to you, rather than trying to change that opportunity to fit what you might believe are your best skill sets."[4]

Zell had also built a property portfolio that was fully capable of realizing his long-held ethos of offering more for less, something he felt would be a key differentiator in the industry, and help him make more money. He had built a gargantuan enterprise that put him in the powerful position to negotiate bulk prices from suppliers on everything from toilet tissue and paper towels to light bulbs.

Never content to sit on a status quo, even of his own making, over the years Zell experimented with various management initiatives, always looking to extract maximum results from as little cost as possible. Some of his schemes worked to better effect than others. Among his many plaudits, Zell is largely credited with reinventing modern management of the office building industry, surrounding himself with top-drawer talent with decades of experience in managing buildings.

"When it's all said and done, the real estate industry historically has not focused enough on the importance of customer relationships and customer service," said Zell. "We at Equity Office Properties like to say that our assets are our tenants. We have a five-and-a-half year average exposure to them, and our job is to make optimum use out of that five-and-a-half years."[5]

In fact, Zell initiated a grand experiment, using his service platform as a way to "brand" EOP's buildings. "Branding by definition means that you look at an asset and you have an expected level of service and attention. Responsiveness to the needs or fears of our tenants is a critical element of long-term confidence. There is little doubt in my mind that on a national basis we are beginning to see the branding of real estate," Zell predicted.[6]

Alas, his prediction was never realized. Real estate was, is, and apparently will forever be a local business; tenants never fully grasped the advantages of being in an Equity building as opposed to other buildings. Ultimately it came down to their pocketbooks, the dollars and cents of the price per square foot they would pay when it came time for lease renewal or expansion.

Though his deal-making prowess had shown through over the past two decades, like many entrepreneurs who are never content to sit on the sidelines, Zell has been equally prone to the occasional error in judgment. At least it can be argued that he is never afraid to try something new.

A MAJOR MISCUE

Warren E. "Ned" Spieker is a lanky, easygoing Californian. From humble beginnings in 1970, just outside San Jose, Spieker stole a page from Zell's own playbook—he was absolutely in the right place, right time.

By the turn of the millennium, the region quickly became the world's technology headquarters, with the likes of Microsoft, Intel, and Cisco. By early 2001, Spieker had built one of the country's largest office REITs out of office and industrial properties in northern California and the Pacific Northwest, with a market value of over $7 billion. And that was enough to attract the attention of one Sam Zell.

In his zeal to build an instant power base in the region, Zell was persuaded to take a rare, calculated gamble on Silicon Valley real estate. A year after the technology stock bubble had inflated nearly to its bursting point with the NASDAQ reaching an all-time high of 5,132.52 on March 10, 2000, EOP purchased Spieker for a whopping $7.3 billion.

The deal was valued at a slight premium to Spieker's share price, and for once, Zell seemed to be buying just as prices were peaking. Why? Spieker was ready to sell and Zell needed coverage in the Northwest office market. After Spieker received an offer to buy out his company, he decided to call Zell to test his interest. Even Spieker had seen that being bigger meant long-term survival, and at fifty-six years of age, it was time to start cashing in after thirty years of work.

In typical Zell style, the deal was encased in secrecy. He shuns layers of managers that might come between himself and the outcome he seeks. In this case, he communicated directly with Spieker to hammer out the details. Amazingly, the deal was done in only sixty days, with no leaks to the outside world.

By now it was difficult to see how EOP could get much larger, considering it owned 616 buildings with 124 million square feet. That was roughly equivalent to owning 32 Sears Towers. But only two months later, Zell was less concerned about EOP's growth and more concerned about its survival. The bursting of the fragile dot-com bubble in 2000 followed by the dramatic events of September 11, 2001, left many overnight billionaires virtually penniless. Over the next twelve months, the NASDAQ lost more than 62 percent of its value, falling to an all-time low of 1,108.49 on October 10, 2002. One bright spot in the action—EOP became the first REIT named to the Standard & Poor's 500 Index in October 2001.

Though Zell admitted he knew little about technology or dot-coms and only followed online news when it appeared on his Bloomberg desktop terminal, he was soon to find out much more than he ever wanted to know about being ahead of his time, often referred to as being on "the bleeding edge." Through 2002 and 2003, the economic recession lingered on. And the previously insatiable expansion by dot-coms led to a severe hangover of excess office space that would take years to release.

Commercial property values in California hit the skids thanks to corporate cutbacks and a major California power crisis. Rents in the critical Silicon Valley market plummeted to just $25 a foot in the first quarter of 2004 from $55 in the fourth quarter of 2000. Still, Zell was unapologetic and stubborn in refusing to admit that he might have made an error in judgment. "As ill-timed as the Spieker transaction might appear, I don't think you necessarily get to pick the time that you get to dominate the intellectual capital of the United States," he noted.[7]

While facing multiple challenges on many fronts, Zell's multitasking capabilities and management moxie were also being put to the test as EOP experienced its own internal upheavals. CEO Tim Callahan resigned in April 2002 for undisclosed reasons, taking with him a nice $1.65 million in "separation pay." Zell quickly assumed the reins as president and CEO. That same month, EOP entered the prestigious Fortune 500 for the first time, ranked at number 491.

In a bold move, Zell tapped Richard Kincaid, EOP's boyish forty-one-year-old chief operating officer and a Zell protégé, as the company's new leader in November 2002. Kincaid had cut his teeth at Zell's privately run Equity Group Investments from 1990 to 1995. After joining EOP as chief financial officer and chief operating officer, he helped engineer a dramatic reshaping of the company's internal organizational structure.

For every step forward, however, there was at least one step back, thanks to the difficulty of the mounting challenges. The lingering economic recession was forcing companies to cut back on office space, and lease terminations—in which tenants give back their space to landlords—became commonplace. Zell's plan to woo and coddle tenants with loving care and attention took a backseat to harsh economic realities.

No longer capable of proactive engagement, ultimately EOP found itself in the awkward position of playing defense. To help prop up its stock price, EOP began to repurchase its own stock in August 2002. In all, EOP increased its share repurchase program from $200 million to $1.6 billion in November 2005.

At the same time, Zell quickly put EOP in full-tilt sales mode. In 2002, EOP sold $500 million worth of buildings in secondary markets like Nashville and Charlotte. In 2003, EOP sold fifty-five buildings for $933.1 million, completely exiting five office markets. In 2004, it sold off $684 million in properties. For all of 2005, EOP sold $2.7 billion of assets. In 2006, it sold off another $2.2 billion. Along the way, Zell completely abandoned several of EOP's largest markets, including Atlanta and Dallas.

But EOP was not alone. The public market giveth and sometimes it taketh away. Many REITs saw their share prices cut in half through the early part of the decade, never to recover to what they viewed as true market value. And more and more frequently, Zell squabbled publicly with Wall Street analysts, comparing them to nincompoops. "How can an educated analytical community be so far off?" Zell asked. "I think the real-estate community has dramatically suffered from the fact that we've had a relatively poor analytical following and our analytical savants have come to the table with very significant opinions that ignore reality."[8]

As an entrepreneur and a risk-taker, Zell often eschews the built-in microscope that comes with life as a public company, where quarterly results are virtually all that matter. Deliver a steady stream of earnings performance, with no hiccups or surprises, and you're swimming in peaches and cream. Don't make your numbers, and you suffer the ignominy of being called out on the investor conference call.

Unfortunately, by early 2006, EOP's numbers were still heading in the wrong direction as deep cracks began to appear in its financial foundation. Wall Street analysts were less than enamored with the company's performance. Measured against its peer group, EOP was not going gangbusters. Boston Properties, another major office REIT that went public a month after EOP, produced a 131 percent return over five years compared to EOP's anemic 26 percent return.

Most alarming was EOP's plan to cut its annual stock dividend by 34 percent for the first quarter of 2006. For REITs, that's serious news, for they are required by law to pay out at least 95 percent of their taxable income as dividends. Four years earlier, Zell had termed EOP's $2 dividend as "inviolate." But EOP had been selling off assets since the second half of 2003 just to meet its dividend payments.

As luck and good economic timing would have it, Zell's pain was short-lived. Starting in late 2004, U.S. commercial real estate markets were booming again. Soon the exuberance would bring much needed relief to EOP's flagging financials.

Still smarting from an undervalued stock price, and with the investment world awash in private equity capital, Zell started listening to the growing chorus of contrarian voices in his head. After all, he still owned more office space than any of his more famous name-brand peers—Donald Trump, Mortimer Zuckerman, or Leona Helmsley. Famously sensing a coming downturn in the markets, Zell knew it was time to sell. Perhaps the tagline of a 2006 Equity Office corporate brochure told the real story: "Right Place, Right Time."

6

BIDDING WAR

CORPORATE TAKEOVERS ARE undeniably fascinating. Call it corporate theater. Or a big-monied soap opera entitled *As the Merger Turns*. After all, they often feature strong personalities, power, greed, and intrigue. And, oh yes, money, lots of money. As in billions of dollars in cold hard cash.

Nearly twenty years after the largest takeover in corporate history—the $25 billion RJR Nabisco purchase by Wall Street leveraged buyout artists Kohlberg, Kravis, & Roberts in 1988—the blow-by-blow account of the $39 billion auction and sale of Zell's Equity Office Properties is fascinating stuff.

This battle pitted two of the most dominant financiers in the world against one another. On one side was the richest man on Wall Street, the Ivy League–schooled Stephen A. Schwarzman and his buttoned-down, Park Avenue–based private equity shop known as the Blackstone Group. On the other sat a longtime friend of Zell's, Steven Roth, the street-smart, Brooklyn-born, tough-talking head of Vornado Realty Trust, another major office building owner. Each sought Sam's bulked-up prize, but after four months of bidding one-upmanship, only one would reward Zell with the billions he was seeking.

While real estate industry veteran Roth preferred to deal with the day-to-day bidding process himself, Schwarzman tapped into his own resident real estate deal maker, Jonathan Gray, to handle Blackstone's bidding. Gray, a Chicago native, had earned a well-deserved reputation for creating enormous value for Blackstone. No major deal involving commercial real estate happened without his knowing about it, or instigating it.

Gray had his eye on EOP for some time. He well understood the growing disconnect between the company's basement-level stock price and the value of its prime office buildings, which were literally climbing sky-high. He knew this firsthand after buying two other office REITs, Trizec Properties Inc. and CarrAmerica Realty Corp.

Still, Gray was slightly distracted as the fall of 2006 approached. He was smack-dab in the middle of his own megadeal, a $20 billion takeover of Hilton Hotels Corporation. When that deal ran into a few snags (Blackstone later reconstituted the deal and bought Hilton for $26 billion in July 2007), he was ready to track down an offer for EOP.

Though he knew it would be a megadeal of extreme proportions, Blackstone had the clout to raise whatever money it would take to buy the company. And Gray's experience told him there would be plenty of ready bidders salivating at the prospect of snapping up EOP's iconic buildings if they were ever to go up for sale.

Then and there, the hunt was on. And this time, Zell would be in the enviable position of seller rather than buyer.

KNOCKING ON THE DOOR

Potential suitors first flirted with EOP at the end of 2005. EOP's stock price was hovering around $30 a share, and like many REIT executives, Zell was openly perplexed at the low valuation.

While Wall Street stock analysts were certainly walking all over themselves to see who could cut the most value from Zell's real estate holdings, he was mindful of the public nature of his businesses and the thousands of shareholders who owned a stake in them. That helps explain why he shunned takeover defenses in any of his companies. And he believed that if someone made what he referred to as a "Godfather" offer, or one that was substantially higher than your projected valuation, then it had to be seriously considered.

Zell's own internal analysis valued EOP at a share price in the high-$30 range. And he's a stickler for knowing the value of his holdings on a moment's notice. That explains why valuations are conducted about every ninety days on all of his real estate companies. This became an especially important point during the EOP sale process.

Over the next few months, a series of potential buyers came knocking, but none reached the formal offer stage. Then a breakthrough came in August 2006 when Blackstone's Gray approached Zell's advisors at Merrill Lynch about making a deal. Gray was proposing to buy EOP for $40 to $42 a share and sell off a third of the assets to another large public office company.

The overture drew a tepid response. "Our attitude has always been that if an offer came and was marginally better, that's probably not something we would consider," said Zell. Still, the offer effectively meant that EOP was "in play," meaning it would quickly draw attention from other buyers. Blackstone knew this, and Zell began his favorite deal dance, playing hard to get. Remember that the commercial real estate markets were at their absolute historical zenith, and Zell played his hunch that Blackstone, and hopefully a few other buyers, would continue to dance with him, but on his terms.

His hunch was right. Three months later, Blackstone came knocking again, this time with an offer of $47.50 a share, all in cash. Zell was openly shocked at the number and the EOP board agreed it was worth pursuing. Zell and Gray began a series of nonstop negotiations, which produced a price of $48.50 per share. On November 19, 2006, Zell and Blackstone signed their merger agreement and set a closing date of February 7.

While the outside world marveled at the size of Blackstone's offer and the surety of its purchase, Zell knew better. He wanted to press for more. To Zell the experienced deal maker, this was only the beginning of what he hoped would be a protracted auction process that would extract even more value not only for himself but also EOP's shareholders.

Over the intervening months, Zell fully expected to see more bidders step up to the plate. The goal was to create an auction among highly competitive bidders, which would ultimately yield a higher purchase price. But even if he didn't get a penny more, cashing out at $48.50 was not so bad.

Zell's negotiating style is best described as blunt. He dissects the facts and figures, and he also looks for any angle, any loophole, that he can leverage to his advantage.

In this instance, Zell put his legal training to good use, giving himself an enviable bargaining position thanks to a key provision he installed in the Blackstone agreement. Every megadeal includes what is known as a breakup fee, or a negotiated sum that the seller (Zell) agrees to pay the original suitor—in this case Blackstone— in the event that another bidder offers a better deal and the new purchase is finalized. It amounts to compensation for the original bidder's time and expense, sort of a salve for having to walk away.

"The real negotiation at that point was not so much about price but about a focus on the breakup fee," Zell noted. Normal breakup fees in merger transactions average between 2 percent and 3 percent of the sale price, an amount that is significant enough to discourage the seller from siding with a competing buyer. But the fact that Blackstone clearly wanted what Zell was selling more than he wanted to sell it allowed him to strike a hard bargain, amounting to only a .91 percent breakup fee.

Zell's unique ability to assess every angle of a transaction brought into sharp focus two key points. First, in Blackstone he was facing a tough negotiator and a well-connected Wall Street powerhouse. Zell was well aware that Blackstone had the ability to impede an auction if it so desired, simply by tying up monies that potential bidders would need.

"Now I'm sure there is no question that Blackstone is above reproach," Zell opined in his typical tongue-in-cheek manner. "The fact that they decided to finance their $32 billion offer with 16 banks at $2 billion instead of 3 banks at $10 billion might have suggested perhaps they were thinking that if they could get 16 banks for $2 billion each there weren't going to be a lot of fucking banks left to finance a competitor. At a certain point in the transaction I was forced to remind them of that provision."[1] This included a tense face-to-face breakfast with Blackstone's Jonathan Gray in New York.

Zell also carefully stacked most of the cards in his favor, as he turned up the pressure on Blackstone with a strict confidentiality agreement. Immediately following its purchase, Blackstone was keen to sell off many of EOP's buildings as quickly as possible to pay down the exorbitant debt Blackstone was heaping on the company. Initially, Zell prohibited Blackstone from talking with potential buyers to prearrange sales ahead of the closing, because he felt that would taint the sales process.

As the clock ticked nearer to the February 7 closing deadline, Zell started getting antsy. December came and went with no serious counteroffers. Not content to wait, Zell's inborn sense of humor and proclivity for the unconventional had him goading his old friend Roth, at Vornado, to step into the bidding war. Roth and Zell had held numerous conversations over previous months about merging their companies, but now Zell needed to see some concrete interest. He sent Roth a cheeky note, reading, "Roses are red, violets are blue, I hear a rumor, is it true?"

It was a simple tactic that seemed oddly out of place for a multi-billion-dollar deal. Yet it was indicative of Zell's direct style. And it worked. The next day, Roth replied, "Roses are red, violets are blue, I love you Sam, my bid is $52."[2] That $52 a share offer was structured with 60 percent of the purchase in cash and 40 percent in Vornado stock. Roth would keep half of EOP's buildings on the East Coast and divvy up the rest to investment partners Starwood Capital Group and Walton Street Capital.

Unfortunately for Vornado, the calendar read January 17, and the February 7 deadline for closing Blackstone's deal was only three short weeks away.

Fortunately for Zell, he now had another offer with which to twist Blackstone's arm to extract a higher bid. He gave Gray a quick call and suggested that Blackstone increase its bid to $54 all cash with no contingencies. In exchange, he would raise the breakup fee to $500 million. "We convinced them that was a prudent decision on their part, amended the agreement, increased the breakup fee and we got the deal to $54 all cash," said Zell.[3]

It appeared that Vornado was punted out of the game. But only three days before the deal closing, all hell broke loose. As the rest of the world was enjoying Super Bowl Sunday, just as the second half of the game was starting, Zell received a surprise call from Roth—Vornado threw a $56 offer on the table. Though the price was certainly right, time was about to run out. Because Vornado was a publicly traded company, it would take quite a bit longer to approve the purchase, including approval from the Securities and Exchange Commission.

Zell's hand, however, had not been fully played. He knew full well how much Blackstone coveted EOP's assets. He pushed the envelope, and Gray's patience, to the wall, telling Gray he would hike the breakup fee to $700 million and allow Blackstone to start talking to potential buyers.

Ultimately Vornado bowed out of the contest, and the deal closed at $55.50, all cash. In the end, Zell had managed to extract a 15 percent premium from Blackstone over its original bid months earlier. And his legend reached epic proportions. "In a postmortem, it is all about certainty. It is all about eliminating the options and intelligently assessing risk as it should be," said Zell matter-of-factly.[4]

It is also about great timing. This high-stakes game of corporate chicken was conducted during the height of the lending frenzy brought on by Wall Street's powerhouses. Consider its dynamics. Here was a whopping $39 billion deal, the largest corporate takeover in history at the time, in which the buyer, Blackstone, put up only $3 billion of equity—less than 10 percent of the final purchase price. There was $32 billion of debt, and the investment banks put up $5 billion of bridge or short-term equity.

In the end, Blackstone earned a hefty 60 percent return for its investors. At the same time, Zell looked like both a genius for selling at the top of the real estate markets, but also like a fool for allowing anyone other than him to earn a 60 percent profit. This is a point that Zell quickly dismissed, noting that Blackstone had taken an extraordinarily bold risk to earn its reward.

Zell saw a narrow window of opportunity to quickly reap what he had spent decades sowing. He was proven right, as less than a year after the EOP sale, the financial markets had begun to go into a full lockdown mode.

WORK TO DO

Spending $39 billion was surprisingly easy in early 2007, but recouping it would be another story, and Jonathan Gray had some work to do to beat the ticking debt clock. To make the EOP deal work, he was arranging piecemeal sales of some of the company's prime assets even before it closed. Legendary New York developer Harry Macklowe purchased eight of EOP's buildings in the Manhattan office market for $7 billion on the same day Gray was closing Blackstone's deal to buy EOP. That bit of gambit saved Blackstone some $200 million in New York City and state transfer taxes.

The ink had barely dried on the sales contract before Gray was playing sales director for the bidders salivating for a piece of EOP's pie. First in line was Macklowe. That deal would go south quickly on him, though, as the commercial real estate markets took a nosedive in late 2007 and Macklowe was forced to sell his prizes at a significant loss.

Gray continued to up the pace, taking advantage of the red-hot office sales market to unload 19 buildings in Washington, D.C., and 17 more in Seattle to Beacon Capital Advisors for $6.35 billion. Another group of 17 buildings in Portland, Oregon, were sold to Shorenstein Co. for $1.2 billion. In less than a month after closing the largest corporate takeover in history, Gray had managed to pay down more than a quarter of the debt. Six months after the closing, he had orchestrated the sale of more than 60 percent of the assets and recouped 70 percent of its purchase price.

For Zell, the Blackstone transaction finally vindicated his

much-maligned purchase of Spieker Properties in 2001. By selling out, all of EOP's holdings were essentially valued at $54 a share versus the $29 a share he paid for Spieker. At least that's one way of looking at it.

After the Blackstone merger, even though Zell's pockets had been richly lined with preposterous amounts of cash—an estimated $1.1 billion—he was not shy to lament on the frothy nature of the proceedings.

To Zell, the demand for his properties had little basis in reality. It was more a function of who had the most money to spend and who could spend it the fastest. Though Zell had established a track record for owning quality properties, it mattered little to the market of early 2007. The frenetic pace of deal making and the long lines of potential buyers left little time to actually see what was inside. Instead, it was all about doing the deal.

7

SAM'S WAY (OR THE HIGHWAY)

OVERNIGHT, IT SEEMED, Sam Zell had become a business icon. Thanks to the blockbuster deal, his name appeared in headlines on the front pages of every major daily newspaper. Suddenly he was regarded with adulation. He saw what others could not. One pundit even noted that his reputation had suddenly been elevated to super-hero status and that he could leap over his own tall buildings with a single bound. The only thing missing was a costume change—Zell could easily wear a "Super Sam" outfit complete with a red S on his chest.

That bit of fun might be over the top for most corporate execu-tives, but put nothing past Sam Zell. To be sure, philosophy 101 teaches that a razor-thin line exists between genius and madness. Which characterization best fits Zell? That depends on whom you ask, but he is sanguine, and downright comfortable, within his quirky persona. He proudly admits to an abundance of self confi-dence, which allows him to continually push the limits of what he views as possible.

One thing that can be said of Zell with absolute certainty—you always know where he stands and what he's thinking. And just in case you don't, he often reminds you with a curt "Do you want me to speak slower?" followed by a quick and condescending smirk. He almost never keeps his opinions to himself, which is part of what makes him so interesting to so many people.

"It's a combination of his intelligence—he clearly is brilliant—and his filter is less high-strung than others so he's willing to say what's on his mind while most of us have impulse control," said Jonathan Kempner, former president of the National Multihousing Council and the Mortgage Bankers Association. "He's delightful and insightful and therefore he's quite compelling. He also looks like he's straight out of central casting."[1]

SALESMAN SAM

Adult readers of the Dr. Seuss book *Green Eggs and Ham* usually have one of two takeaways after poring over the whimsical classic of children's literature. The first is admiration for lead character Sam's salesmanship abilities and his ultimate success. The second is loathing for his persistence in pushing a product on an obviously annoyed, bewildered, and downright hapless customer, a negative characterization to which nearly everyone can relate.

As another salesman Sam, Zell more closely aligns himself with the former interpretation of that story than the latter. He relishes the art of the sale and always has, viewing it as a kind of purist art form that only a few have mastered, including himself.

Zell even takes issue with noted playwright and fellow University of Michigan alum Arthur Miller. In his highly acclaimed play *Death of a Salesman*, Miller portrays the stereotypical salesman, lead character Willy Loman, as a down-on-his-luck, miserable wretch of a human being trudging through life. According to Zell, however, salesmanship is a gift that should be revered, and contrary to popular belief, "nothing is bought and everything is sold." Ultimately, he believed his ability to communicate and gain followers was one of the great keys to his success.

Zell so highly values the art of communication that he insists it is essential to the making of a true leader. "I realized that being able to sell your ideas is what leadership is really all about. People will follow ideas. People don't follow people. And your ability to define and delineate your ideas, to bring them to a level of simplicity so that others can both understand and buy in, is an extraordinary asset and a requirement to achieve true leadership."

Though he is a committed nonconformist, one might get the sense that Zell is fearless. He insists quite the opposite is true. "At times going against conventional wisdom is painful, lonely, and for sure creates all kinds of self-doubt and fear. I might add that fear is an extraordinarily healthy characteristic. I don't do business with anybody who's not afraid, and I won't hire anybody who is confident to the point where fear is not very close to the surface. I've often said that fear and courage are cousins and very closely related."[2]

TAKE ME ON

Often it is difficult to know exactly where Sam the Salesman and Sam the Person diverge. In speeches, he expounds. In private meetings, he is thoughtful and even congenial. So which is the "real" Sam Zell? Is he just playing the corporate clown to stir up the troops and have a bit of fun?

"My job is to ask questions," he said. "And sometimes I'm going to be right. But I promise you I will for sure be wrong sometimes, and maybe more, but I just want people to take me on. I've spent my whole career trying to build up people around me who will take me on, because that's the ultimate test of whether the ideas are right or not."[3]

For many, however, taking on Sam Zell, the man of many contradictions, has proven anything but a pleasant experience. "At the *L.A. Times,* he brought people together and said they could ask him anything, but as soon as anybody did, he flew off," said Kevin Roderick, a twenty-year veteran of the *Los Angeles Times* and founder of an all-things-L.A. Web site called LA Observed. "That was a very deflating moment at the *L.A. Times,* because then they saw that he was not a guy who had their best interests at heart. He was not very interested in journalism. He was not there to make the newspapers better or improve journalism. But also there was a sense that he was . . . not what he seems to be. He's just an angry little man to some people."[4]

Angry or not, the business record, at least, indicates that Zell has been right a lot more often than he has been wrong. That's not to say he hasn't had some spectacular blunders. One notable bogey was his investment in American Classic Voyages Co. Saddled with a hefty debt load, management bungles, and a catastrophic drop in tourism following the September 11, 2001, terrorist attacks, the company filed for Chapter 11 protection in October 2001 with only $37.4 million in assets and $452.8 million in debts.

Surprisingly, Zell lost more than $100 million of his own money in the deal, but U.S taxpayers lost far more, to the tune of more than $350 million. In the mid-1990s, American Classic lobbied the U.S. Maritime Administration to build two 1,900-room cruise ships, the first to be built in the United States in fifty years. Zell received more than $1 billion in government loans to build the ships, but the bankruptcy filing mothballed those plans. Zell and American Classic then incurred the wrath of one U.S. Senator John McCain, who had repeatedly warned against using government funding for the project.

When you live the point-man, risk-taking life that is Sam Zell's, you're bound to meet failure. "He is not shy about admitting he is wrong," said colleague Peter Linneman. "But he is not quick to admit he is wrong either, and that's a good trait, because if you're constantly changing your mind, it probably means you've changed your mind a lot of times when you shouldn't have, and you're blowing with the wind as it were. There is a belief in the fundamentals. He'll say he's in the business of trying to be right sixty-five percent of the time as an investor. Barry Bonds or Willie Mays were legends because they hit .330, and in the investment world, if you can hit .650 or so, you're a legend."[5]

Other Zell alumni swear that their years with Zell were career changers. Many are highly pedigreed, with MBAs from Harvard and other highbrow institutions. Stephen Quazzo and Randy Rowe, both Harvard grads, were on Zell's original team in the mid-1980s, helping set up the Zell/Merrill Lynch investment funds, as well as Zell's follow-on Equity branded companies.

"What I learned the most being there was what it takes to be a principal," said Quazzo, who heads Chicago-based Transwestern Investment Company, which has invested more than $10 billion in commercial real estate. "I had come from the investment banking side at Goldman Sachs, where you're advising clients, making recommendations, and performing valuations. But when you're on the other side and you're the owner or you're making a decision to invest and putting your own capital at risk, the dynamics are a lot different. Working with Sam's organization, you understand how truly capital-intensive real estate is and how labor-intensive it is. Among the many things he's particularly adept at is being a good risk manager and being able to evaluate downside. He's a quick read on any potential decision and being around him all that time and seeing that, well, hopefully some of it rubbed off."[6]

For Rowe, chairman of real estate investment firm Green Courte

Partners in suburban Chicago, it was all about the constant intellectual challenge. "I can't imagine a better place to have gone to learn real estate. I considered it my postgraduate, postgraduate degree in joining Sam in 1989, given what was going on in the markets and given that securitization was coming about and there were going to be new vehicles and approaches. It was a very exciting time, very fast-paced, intellectually very stimulating. Sam is a brilliant guy and has a number of sayings that as you get older you have more appreciation for. Things like, 'Let the asset be what it wants to be.' Or 'If you're not the lead dog, the view never changes.'

"Obviously Sam loves what he's doing or he wouldn't be doing it. He is an extremely unique individual in that he can take almost any business and have an impact and make it better," said Rowe. "He would tell you that the concepts are pretty consistent. Ultimately everything is driven by cash flow. If you focus on what the real cash flows are and what you can do to impact those cash flows, that ultimately is what creates value. Whether it is a corporate-style business or something totally unrelated to real estate or not, the basic business concepts are consistent. That includes incentivizing and rewarding people."[7]

Of course brilliance is one thing, but demeanor is another. And Zell's has certainly been questioned over his forty-five-plus years in business. It's not surprising that he has won his fair share of detractors. His abrasive nature and do-it-now mentality do not endear him to everyone, which explains why so many of his inner circle have had to develop rather thick skins.

SHUTTING OUT THE NOISE

To keep his business acumen razor sharp, Zell insists that briefings be kept to a single page, no matter how complicated the deal or issue. Anything more is summarily dismissed. This is not a case of attention deficit disorder, but more a practical realization that his insanely busy schedule requires quick thinking and steady focus.

For Zell, simple ideas and concepts have always yielded the highest rewards. "Having conviction means that you can shut out the noise."

Zell has the experience of having seen several business cycles, from the go-go real estate boom of the eighties to the dot-com era of the late nineties. And he has stayed true to the belief that if it looks too good to be true, it probably is worth avoiding. He has resisted the temptation to run with the herd. Or better yet, the lemmings.

MOTIVATED MAN

Zell is never one to stand still. In fact he openly detests what the rest of Corporate America views as downtime. What some call manic, Zell terms motivation, though he can't credit some mystical formula he ingested as a child as the root cause of his drive to overachieve.

While most businesspeople are raised on the notion that goals are set to be achieved, Zell says goals are just bumps in a longer career road. It's that motivation factor again, and for anyone cruising along the twists and turns of Zell's career highway, there are telltale signposts everywhere, the most prominent being "No Limits."

Rather than having some advanced type of attention deficit disorder, Zell insists that he is just constantly eager to learn and to do, rather than sitting pat with what he has already learned in life. He is intensely curious, craving to discover the next bit of knowledge that will put him ahead. Combine that trait with his motivated nature, and he can often be described as a sort of whirling dervish.

While Zell is known as a global purveyor of four-letter words, one that he tosses around a lot, *risk,* is less offensive. An entrepreneur, he opines, embraces risk in their soul. Still, he seems to have a chip in his brain that moderates the actual degree of risk he is willing to chance. His root philosophy is to strike gold around 70 percent of the time, leaving another 30 percent to play high-stakes poker.

NEXT!

Like all businesspeople, Zell lives in a world that is closely tied to economic conditions. And certainly the economy was in full-on growth mode in 2006 and early 2007, the halcyon days when deals like the Equity Office sale were doable, and worries about tomorrow were nearly nonexistent.

As late as September 2007, only seven months after his Equity Office sell-off, Zell viewed collateralized loan and debt obligations as infantile prodigies of Wall Street's latest fascination with financial engineering. While still untested, to him they represented yet another means to an end, potentially powerful new sources of investment capital.

And oh how they would be tested. According to the National Bureau of Economic Research, the U.S. recession actually started in December 2007. For once, Zell's prognostications failed him as he did not grasp the full magnitude of the coming economic storm. He largely blamed the crisis on a lack of confidence rather than on a lack of capital, dismissing the gathering clouds over the world economy as little more than an inconvenient, negative perception perpetuated by off-the-mark media reports. At the time, he thought a turnaround might appear in as little as three to six months.

Unfortunately for Zell, the economic crisis would grow far worse than he imagined, leading to the worst downturn since the Great Depression in the 1930s. And just on the horizon lay his date with Tribune Company.

8

OPEN KIMONO

SAM ZELL IS proud of the fact that his office door has never been closed. "Open kimono!" he shouted, referring to his insistence on clear and visible transparency in business dealings and sharing of information within his own company. Given his disdain for politically correct corporate colloquialisms, it's perhaps not surprising that he loves to spring that phrase on unsuspecting ears.

While still in the final throes of cashing out on his sale of Equity Office to Blackstone, the rumblings inside the confines of Zell's office began reverberating through the halls at Equity Group Investments. Zell was simultaneously exploring yet another gargantuan deal, this time in an industry he barely knew, but one with far-reaching influence and even, in his eyes anyway, huge profit potential.

His next and most challenging target was Chicago-based Tribune Company, one of the leading media conglomerates in the world. Tribune is the second-largest newspaper publisher in the world. The company reached more than 80 percent of U.S. households through newspaper publishing, television and radio broadcasting, and the Internet, with operations concentrated in the nation's three largest markets: New York, Los Angeles, and Chicago. Tribune Company had three main divisions:

Tribune Publishing: Owned the *Chicago Tribune, Los Angeles Times, Baltimore Sun, Orlando Sentinel, Hartford Courant.*

Tribune Broadcasting: Owned twenty-three major-market television stations, including WGN in Chicago and KXLA in Los Angeles. Its programming division, Tribune Entertainment, produced syndicated staples *South Park, Family Feud, Soul Train,* and *Candid Camera.*

Tribune Interactive: Owned leading Web sites CareerBuilder .com, Cars.com, and Apartments.com.

Tribune even had a stake in Major League Baseball. Back in 1981, it purchased the often loved yet much maligned Chicago Cubs franchise, along with their stately landmark home, Wrigley Field, for only $20.5 million.

Founded in 1847, Tribune was one of the oldest and most closely watched of American media companies. With the start of the new millennium, however, Tribune's fortunes went on a roller-coaster ride, marked by ongoing management changes and wild gyrations in its financial performance.

Sitting in his Chicago office, Zell was catching wind of Tribune's travails, thanks to William Pate, one of his top lieutenants. Pate had an incessant habit of keeping his ear to the ground, searching for the equivalent of corporate roadkill.

A takeover of Tribune would not only be another tall mountain to climb, it would require a mountain of new debt the likes of which even someone as rich as Zell had never financed. It would also put his hands on the true levers of power, the media. Little did he know that Tribune's travails were about to go on public display.

TUMULTUOUS HISTORY

Tribune's own storied and tumultuous history speaks volumes about the vagaries of conducting business in the modern-day media world. It is littered with the successes and failures of strong leaders, with family squabbles, with economic challenges, and with corporate gamesmanship. In this sense, Tribune during the upcoming Zell regime mirrored previous decades of upheaval and near-constant change.

Not unlike Zell's own blockbuster deal for Tribune in 2007, the turn of the new millennium saw Tribune buy out Los Angeles–based rival newspaper publisher Times Mirror. In June 2000, Tribune paid a whopping $8.3 billion in cash and stock, making it the largest publishing deal in history. By most accounts, the price, at $95 a share, was extremely rich. But one group in particular did not mind that one bit.

Throughout its long history, Times Mirror was clearly run as a business first and as a journalistic enterprise second. Like many American publishing businesses, members of the founding family held a major stake in the company and were heavily involved in running its operations. In the case of Times Mirror, a series of trusts named after the founding Chandler family were in place. These trusts would effectively control the company starting in 1938, and ultimately would play a pivotal role in the future direction of Times Mirror.

In 1964, the trusts were enormously enriched when Times Mirror became the first newspaper-based media company to list its stock on the New York Stock Exchange. All was rosy for decades as the Chandlers sat contentedly on their mound of cash. And then Tribune came calling with an offer Times Mirror couldn't refuse.

At the time of the Tribune takeover, many Los Angeles locals reacted with disdain at the "sellout" to the Chicago interloper. It was much the same way they reacted years later when Zell came to town—with outrage and outbursts of "how dare they sell out," to the Midwest of all places. Old grudges apparently die hard.

With the purchase, Tribune took over four major newspapers—the *Los Angeles Times, Newsday,* the *Baltimore Sun,* and the *Hartford Courant,* plus three smaller papers in Allentown, Pennsylvania, and Stamford and Greenwich, Connecticut. The deal leapfrogged Tribune into the company of such stellar newspaper publishers as Gannett Co. Inc. and Knight Ridder Inc.

Tribune CEO John Madigan reasoned that "synergies" could be realized between the major-market newspaper, television, and online properties. He envisioned the creation of a national advertising network that could reap significantly higher revenues from selling advertisers the depth and breadth of the country. Thus Tribune Media Net Inc. was born.

But Tribune faced a massive debt load after the acquisition, and divested several properties worth nearly $3 billion in 2000. It also joined with Knight Ridder to form online employment site Career-Builder Inc.

Still facing $4 billion in debt, Tribune in summer 2001 looked very much like the Tribune of 2008, post–Zell takeover. Tribune Broadcasting head Dennis J. FitzSimons was named president and chief operating officer at the same time the U.S. advertising market began what CEO Madigan called "the worst advertising environment since the Depression." That year Tribune cut 10 percent of its payroll, or more than two thousand employees.

FitzSimons was elevated to the CEO's corner office in early 2003 and months later added the chairman's title to his business card. Tribune continued to experiment with new print vehicles, launching new Chicago and Los Angeles versions of the Spanish-language newspaper *Hoy*. It also created a free weekly tabloid targeting Chicago's rail commuters called *RedEye*.

Advertising growth propelled the company to an astounding operating cash flow of $1.6 billion in 2003, of which $1.3 billion came from the publishing division. But a slumping national economy and rising expenses began taking their toll on Tribune's bottom line in early 2004, as did charges to eliminate six hundred publishing positions. The stock market, too, had been most unkind, depressing Tribune's share prices. During the year, the company repurchased 15 million shares of its own stock to prop up shareholder value.

By April 2005, Tribune's publishing and broadcast revenues had slid to the negative plane of the scale. Even so, only a month later at the company's annual meeting, FitzSimons boldly declared, "The business of local mass media is healthy and has excellent growth potential. Tribune's newspapers and television stations are resilient. We have strong franchises in top markets, and they are critically important to advertisers, consumers, and the communities we serve."[1]

By early 2006, the news had only worsened. In 2005, the Tribune took nearly $80 million in pretax charges, including shutting down its *Los Angeles Times* San Fernando Valley printing facility, and millions in severance charges after it cut eight hundred positions. FitzSimons and company were reeling, and in another desperate bid to prop up Tribune's flagging stock price, FitzSimons announced in late May 2006 that the company would trim $200 million in costs and dig deep into its coffers to buy back up to $2 billion of Tribune stock at $32.50 a share.

THE CHANDLER CHA-CHA

There was just one thing standing in FitzSimons's way. In a board meeting to approve the measure on June 6, the three members associated with the Chandler family trusts, which controlled 12 percent of the company's stock, voted against the move. And with that, the war was on.

Zell well understood the subtle—and not so subtle—motivations that were driving the domineering Chandler family two thousand miles away in Los Angeles. The three Chandler board members vehemently opposed Tribune's proposed stock buyback plan and viewed it as the final straw in their long-running struggle with Tribune management to extract what they viewed as fair value for their ownership stake.

The Chandlers had done well to keep their angst private, but on June 13, 2006, they did the unthinkable. Stealing a page from Zell's own playbook, they unleashed a salvo across the bow of Tribune's boardroom. In plain, often terse language, Chandler family attorney William Stinehart laid out the family's concerns for the first time on public display with an eleven-page invective delivered to Tribune management and unceremoniously filed with the SEC. From the opening paragraphs, the tone was clear:

Dear Directors:

The Chandler Trusts do not intend to tender any shares in response to the tender offer announced by Tribune on May 30, 2006. The Trusts believe that the process by which the offer was presented and considered by the Tribune Board was fundamentally flawed, and that the offer is a purely financial device that fails altogether to

address the real business issues facing Tribune. Prompt
and meaningful strategic action is required to preserve the
premium value of the company's franchises.

As you know, the basic strategic premise of the
Tribune/Times Mirror merger was that the cross-
ownership of multiple premium major media properties
in the nation's three largest media outlets would provide a
platform to produce above-industry performance for both
its newspaper and broadcast assets and for strong growth
in interactive and other media opportunities. This strategy
has failed and the regulatory change anticipated at the
time of the merger to make legal the permanent cross-
ownership of certain key assets has not occurred. Over the
past two years, Tribune has significantly underperformed
industry averages and there is scant evidence to suggest the
next two years will be any different. Clearly, it is time for
prompt, comprehensive action.[2]

The Chandlers laid out their opinion, that the company's publishing and broadcast operations should be split into two units, creating opportunities for a sale to maximize their individual values.
Not to mention their stock.

This would be one of the seminal events in the newspaper industry's illustrious 350-year history, as it starkly revealed the landmines
involved in running any modern-day media company. And in a sign
of the economic times, it signaled the end of one of the last true
newspaper dynasties.

Essentially the Trusts made three propositions to Tribune
management—split the newspapers from the broadcasting business
in a tax-free spin-off; sell off the newspapers individually or the company as a whole; and appoint a committee of independent directors
"to oversee a thorough review and evaluation of the management,

business and strategic issues facing Tribune and to promptly execute alternatives to restore and enhance stockholder value."

And where exactly did the Chandlers place the blame for Tribune's decline?

> The gravity of management's failure to address fundamental strategic issues is apparent from the precipitous decline in stock value over the past three and a half years. These results have been disastrous to investors. Over the past two years, the value of Tribune's stock has declined by nearly half. While both the newspaper and broadcasting sectors have been under pressure, Tribune management has had little response.

The Trusts also argued that the breakup value of the company had been largely overlooked or dismissed. Obviously such a breakup would be yet another way for the Trusts to cash out on their long-held Tribune stake. And the Chandlers had obviously done their homework. They surmised that based on several analysts' opinions the company was worth anywhere from $42 per share to $46 per share, which represented a major premium over FitzSimons's plan.

Ultimately, the Chandler Trusts made it clear they were the eight-hundred-pound gorilla that would have sway over the future of the company.

OUTRAGED

Once and for all, and for all to see, the Chandler clan wanted out of Tribune. The bloom had decidedly come off their publishing rose, as the present-day family members now viewed their once bountiful object as an albatross with little in the way of a business future. And the shock waves from the SEC filing reverberated across every media outlet in America.

Not surprisingly, FitzSimons was outraged at this public calling on the carpet, as it represented a boldface repudiation of his management of the company. Caught flat-footed by the indignation of the filing, Tribune issued its own formal response via press release on June 14, 2006, in which FitzSimons tried to vindicate himself and Tribune management. "In a changing media environment, our commitment to quality journalism and service to our communities will continue to be a top priority. We believe Tribune Company has a great future and we are focused on creating long-term value for all of our shareholders, many of whom are employees."[3]

FitzSimons spent the next two months resisting the Chandlers and pursuing his beloved stock-buyback program, to no avail. By September, the program was over and Tribune formally put itself up for sale. More than a year later, after Tribune was sold, FitzSimons described the Chandlers' letter as "the most bogus filing of all time."[4]

When Tribune's board met to determine the fate of the company, the options were few—either break it up into pieces or solicit a buyout. During the meeting, the board voted to ease the path to a sale and formed a special committee of independent directors. At the time, Tribune shares were trading around $30. Wall Street and investors demanded action, and the ice was broken with the 2006 sale of Knight Ridder Inc., the nation's second-largest newspaper chain, to McClatchy Co. for $4.5 billion.

Overseeing the auction was lead independent director William A. Osborn, chairman and a director of Northern Trust Corporation, a $9 billion financial services firm based in Chicago. He would become a pivotal character in the drama that would ensnare Tribune in the long months to come.

The rest of Tribune's special committee included Enrique

Hernandez Jr., chairman, president, CEO, and a director of Inter-Con Security Systems; Betsy D. Holden, a senior advisor to McKinsey & Company; Robert S. Morrison, a former executive of PepsiCo, Quaker Oats Co., and 3M; J. Christopher Reyes, chairman of Reyes Holdings, a food and beverage distributor; Dudley S. Taft, president and CEO of Taft Broadcasting; and Miles D. White, CEO of Abbott Laboratories.

Now they had to focus some serious attention on the task at hand.

9

NEWSPAPER NEOPHYTE

ZELL WAS AN admitted neophyte when it came to understanding the ins and outs of how newspapers operated. But crucially, he did know a thing or two about the basic fundamentals of supply and demand, demographic trend lines, and industries on the wane. He made a successful career out of pumping black gold from dry holes in all kinds of diverse industries, and newspapers were offered up as the next check box on his list of turnaround opportunities.

He was acutely aware of the divisiveness between the *Chicago Tribune* and its Left Coast partner/rival the *Los Angeles Times*. But Zell felt he had the upper hand, thanks to geography alone. After all, Tribune's management team was ensconced only ten blocks from his own sixth floor office in 2 Riverside Drive next to the Chicago River.

Perhaps most important, he empathized with the concept of monetary motivation and recognized how badly the Chandlers wanted to extract a century of value out of their once-prized possession. Though not technically "distressed," the business had all of the earmarks of a potential discount sale. This played perfectly to Zell's "grave dancer" reputation, swooping in to secure a property when it is most vulnerable and finding a logical yet innovative way to turn its fortunes around.

PATE IN PURSUIT

One of Zell's key assets is his ability to surround himself with bright people who are in the business of knowing everything they can about all kinds of diverse industries, including cargo containers, fertilizer, wineries, and real estate. Some of them even know a thing or two about the publishing business.

As soon as Zell spied blood in the water at Tribune, he put William Pate, one of his top lieutenants, in the lead search boat. Though Pate is not well known outside the walls of Equity Group Investments, his role is pivotal, as he runs Equity's non–real estate investment portfolio as chief investment officer.

What Zell lacked in publishing smarts, Pate made up for in spades. It just so happened that the roots of his family tree were buried deep in the business. His father started the *Madill Record*, a weekly paper in the tiny town of Madill, Oklahoma, and Bill Pate is now the third generation of the clan. Two generations of Pates are memorialized in the Oklahoma Press Hall of Fame in Oklahoma City. But tragedy forced the family to sell the *Record* to a family friend, after Pate's older brother was killed in a small-plane crash in 1990.

Bill Pate remembered many long hours of his youth working the printing press, and he saw firsthand how important the local newspaper was to the community. Unlike Zell, Pate said he had "an appreciation for journalism and what journalists do."[1]

Having served him since 1994, Pate also had some keen insight into Zell's core investment philosophies—do your homework to uncover distressed opportunities, manage them to health, and sell them off for a bundle. A Harvard grad with magna cum laude honors, Pate settled in as a financial analyst at a New York investment bank before joining private equity giant Blackstone Group. There he first met Zell. Immediately the two clicked, their philosophies aligned, and he signed on.

Over thirteen years, Pate rose in the ranks to become the top investment officer of Zell's non–real estate investments. Among the companies he helped nurse to health were Covanta Holding Corp., a New Jersey–based trash-to-energy concern, whose sales grew from $531 million to nearly $1.3 billion in just three years.

Early on, Pate, like Zell, well understood the two largest impediments to making Tribune work—the rivalry between Chicago-based Tribune Co. and its largest property, the *Los Angeles Times*, and the need to change the company's culture. Pate also acknowledged that the Tribune buy was not without its perils and pitfalls. "This is a risky deal," Pate said. "If we stumble on this investment, this will mark Sam's career."[2]

ANY BIDDERS? ANYONE?

Through the fall of 2006, Tribune bidders were few and far between, and those expressing any interest were lukewarm on the company. Several well-heeled private equity players took a peek, and the trophy *Los Angeles Times* attracted a few local business magnates who deigned to kick the tires, but serious offers failed to materialize.

Part of the problem was timing. The newspaper advertising market was hitting the skids, and Tribune's financials were tracking on a steeper freefall trajectory than the company's top brass had expected. That minor point set potential bidders on edge.

Tribune's special committee had set a deadline of January 17 for initial bids. Three months later, by March 31, it would declare a winner. By the January deadline, only three major bidding groups had emerged.

First up was a rather dynamic duo comprising two of the West Coast's toughest and most staunchly Democratic businessmen. Supermarket magnate Ronald Burkle was the son of a Los Angeles grocery store manager. He was a self-made man, having run major grocery chains—Dominick's, Fred Meyer, Food 4 Less, and Ralph's. Flamboyant and often dubbed the "Billionaire Playboy," Burkle had a net worth of around $2.5 billion and owned an interest in the National Hockey League's Pittsburgh Penguins.

Burkle was no stranger to deal making. His Yucaipa Companies, a private equity investment firm named after his California home town, had invested in more than thirty companies and banked on none other than Bill Clinton as an advisor. In 1999, Burkle sold Fred Meyer to Kroger for $13.5 billion, pocketing a tidy $1.8 billion in the process.

He also was no stranger to politics and the occasional scandal. Burkle often flexed his political muscle by throwing Democratic fund-raisers at his sprawling Beverly Hills mansion, known as Greenacres. In 2006, he became the subject of a scandal when he accused *New York Post* gossip columnist Jared Paul Stern of trying to extort money in exchange for good press. The columnist was never charged but sued Burkle and Bill and Hillary Rodham Clinton for defamation. That suit was tossed out by a judge in June 2008.

The second partner in this odd-couple arrangement was octo-genarian Eli Broad. Another self-made entrepreneur, Broad is most noted as the founder of Kaufman & Broad Home Corp. (later short-ened to the simpler KB Home), a national home-building firm and the largest builder in California. He also took a turn in the financial services sector as the founder of SunAmerica, a multi-billion-dollar financial services firm specializing in retirement planning.

Broad was much wealthier than Burkle, with an estimated net worth of $6.5 billion, placing him among the wealthiest men in Los Angeles. Broad is a noted civic booster, often contributing to causes that are close to his heart. He was responsible for much of the redevelopment of downtown Los Angeles and has donated some $600 million to the Broad Institute, of the Massachusetts Institute of Technology and Harvard University, for genetic research.

In an unlikely arrangement, these two Los Angeles billionaires met up through a mutual business acquaintance. Their primary interest was in keeping Tribune's crown jewel, the L.A. Times, under local ownership. In November 2006, Burkle and Broad launched a $34 a share bid for the company and began burning up the air miles flying back and forth to Chicago. But as soon as early January, in the wake of weaker than projected financials at Tribune, they had restructured their offer to pay out a $27 per share dividend to shareholders.

Under the Burkle-Broad deal, current shareholders would retain a stake in the new company's stock and thus would reap any gains the duo might manage over time. On the flip side, it would also heap $10.7 billion of new debt on the company, and they did not present a concrete plan for paying off that debt through existing revenue sources.

The second bidder was—surprise!—the Chandler family trusts. On the deadline date of January 17, through attorney Stinehart, they made their first—and, it turned out, only—formal bid to take over Tribune. In essence, they proposed taking control only of Tribune's newspapers, while spinning off the broadcast properties into a separate entity called Tribune Broadcasting. Doing so, they reasoned, would yield a one-time shareholder dividend of $18 to $20 a share.

A third bid group was led by Washington, D.C.–based private investment firm Carlyle Group, which counts among its advisors former presidents George H. W. Bush and Bill Clinton, as well as Louis Gerstner, the former head of IBM. While several private equity firms reviewed Tribune's books, Carlyle was the last of the serious bidders. According to reports at the time, Carlyle saw the most value in Tribune's broadcast properties and made a bid of $4 billion.

Early on, movie mogul David Geffen had also expressed interest in owning the *L.A. Times*. Geffen is the "G" in Dreamworks SKG, a movie production partnership formed by Steven Spielberg, Jeffrey Katzenberg, and Geffen in 1994. He also was a well-known L.A. local, having founded Asylum Records there in 1970 and Geffen Records in 1980.

Geffen's bid for the *Times*? A cool $2 billion. At that point, little did Geffen know that he and the would-be owner of Tribune, Zell, owned homes only minutes apart along the beach in tony Malibu, north of Los Angeles.

Tribune's special committee rejected all three overtures as inadequate. This left Tribune and the Chandlers in the rather unenviable position of needing a new suitor. On February 7, the same day the Equity Office board of directors was voting on the monumental takeover deal with Blackstone, Pate whispered something in Zell's ear that got his attention—the Tribune bids had stalled. They quickly approached the Tribune board with an offer, the terms of which were kept under lock and key. Regardless, it fell on deaf ears.

By early March, Zell was back knocking on Tribune's door with a new bid of $33 a share, along with a uniquely structured employee stock-ownership program, or ESOP. Zell knew that this structure—though fraught with complexity and decidedly unconventional—would appeal to the Chandler family's well-known proclivity for tax avoidance. He had remembered the unique tactic from two years earlier, when he tried it with the purchase of his Covanta Holding Corp. "We came to what we thought was a risk conclusion, and the conclusion was there was a lot of future in the newspaper business and we certainly didn't think it was going down an elevator shaft," said Zell.[3]

In essence, Zell's plan was to convert Tribune into a Subchapter S corporation owned entirely by a new employee stock-ownership plan. The tax advantages of this arrangement were enormous. As an S corporation, Tribune's taxes would be paid by its largest shareholder, the tax-exempt ESOP. So theoretically Tribune's operating profit would be untaxed, freeing up some $300 million in cash for other corporate uses, based on the previous year's results, anyway. Also, gains on the sale of corporate assets would go untaxed if held for at least ten years after the conversion to S corporation status, meaning 2018 or later.

Despite its ingenuity and obvious tax aversion, Zell's bid was met with a cold reception by Tribune's special committee. It appeared almost too complex, and the committee was loath to put the company's employee retirement plan at risk. Essentially the committee was telling Zell they "just didn't get it."

Still, beggars can't be choosers, and time was running out to decide the company's fate, now that the Saturday deadline of March 31 was looming ever so closer. Finally, after six months of tepid response, a funny thing happened on the way to the closing— an auction broke out. Several name-brand corporate chieftains, including GE's former chairman and CEO Jack Welch, News Corp. chairman Rupert Murdoch, and a host of others rattled their sabers and threatened to enter the fray.

At the same time, Tribune's special committee was increasingly skeptical of their own management's ability to implement a sound restructuring plan. So it took it upon itself to reignite discussions with Zell on March 15. For his part, Zell agreed to raise his bid to over $33 a share. It's interesting that Tribune demanded only a measly $25 million breakup fee, a pittance considering the enormity of the deal's potential value.

Zell felt confident enough in his staying power to meet any and all bidders, and with only a week to go until deadline day, he looked on track to seal the deal. At the same time, and unbeknownst to anyone outside their inner circles, Burkle and Broad held private talks with Zell about partnering, making love rather than war, as it were. But Zell declined the offer, saying he would resume talks after he won Tribune, at which point he would entertain selling off pieces of the company.

Feeling spurned, Burkle and Broad decided not to go away quietly into the balmy Los Angeles night. In a letter to Tribune's special committee, they formally objected to what they viewed as favoritism for Zell's plan. Instead, they were ready to initiate their own version of a copycat ESOP package if they were given more time to digest Tribune's financials.

On Thursday March 29, the Burkle-Broad team made good on their word, issuing a revised last-ditch bid amounting to $34 a share, which included a one-time investment of $500 million and the by then obligatory ESOP (proving that there really is no such thing as a new idea). Zell felt that he still had the upper hand, because the special committee had already embraced his pitch and spent countless hours vetting his proposal. Surely they would be less inclined to review a similar offer.

On the fateful decision-crunch weekend, Zell was so confident of his advantage that he decided to stick to his somewhat routine habit of flying out to Los Angeles every other weekend. He valued the chance to relax, and certainly his $14 million John Lautner–designed weekend home, overlooking a rocky point in Malibu, provided a change in scenery. Throughout his many years of travel, it was the one place that Zell could relax, but his peace and quiet on this particular weekend would be broken by incessant interruptions. He was staying tuned to the Tribune proceedings via constant phone updates from Pate. Though physically far from the action, this was a huge deal even by his own standards, and he was totally engaged in the battle.

Just as Zell was heading out of town on Friday, the Tribune board played a bit of a gambit. Faced with two similar bids, they decided to test Zell's resolve and ask him to raise his bid yet again. Zell was now feeling the kind of pressure he normally inflicts on bidders for his own companies. He quickly countered with another offer on Saturday, deliberately testing Tribune's patience by coming in just under the Burkle-Broad bid of $34 a share. On Sunday morning, the Tribune board rejected Zell's offer, asking him to raise it to match Burkle-Broad's. And the board gave him only twelve hours to do so.

When given the news, Zell was incensed and ready to walk away from the bargaining table. He felt he was being played, and yet he still wanted Tribune. To a true corporate turnaround artist, it represented the ultimate test. It was no longer only about the money; it was about the prize itself and what it would mean if he could turn Tribune's fortunes around. His quick analysis of the numbers on a higher bid showed a razor-thin margin of error. He gave himself the green light to proceed.

Reluctantly, late on Sunday, Zell raised his equity commitment from $225 million to $315 million, or the equivalent of $34 a share, equaling the Burkle-Broad bid. In a late-night session at Tribune Tower, the board met at 10:30 P.M. and approved Zell's bid in less than thirty minutes. Pate immediately relayed the good news to Zell via phone. In Los Angeles, it was still only 9:00 P.M., but Zell opted for a quiet celebration with his wife. He had won the prize, but now came the hard part—could he find enough polish to make the trophy shine?

ESOP'S FABLES

Monday, April 2, 2007, dawned cool and crisp over both Chicago and Los Angeles. For Burkle and Broad, the deal was over. If they wanted a piece of Tribune, they would have to deal with Zell. For Zell, the work to close the deal was just getting started. It would take another eight months to complete the complex transaction in December, over a year after Tribune was originally put on the auction block.

The structure of Zell's winning bid was so complicated that it required a three-page press release from Tribune just to explain it all. There was no question, however, that it was a sweet deal for Zell. After all, he had only $315 million of his own skin in the game versus $8.2 billion in new debt. That translates to an equity stake of less than 4 percent. Once again, the grave dancer had danced his jig over an ailing industry. But this time, as he would soon discover, he had to contend with a uniquely pessimistic group of employees, which would make a turnaround of the troubled media company all the more complicated.

First, it would take many months just to explain the ESOP structure to Tribuners. According to Corey Rosen, executive director of the National Center for Employee Ownership, companies controlled through an ESOP structure generally perform better than non-ESOP firms. And though Rosen found nothing "subversive" in Tribune's ESOP, it did seem a poor fit for the economic times. "The vast majority of ESOPs are set up in companies that are successful at the time they are set up and become even more so down the road.

This is unusual in that respect, that you had a company that was in more difficulty at the time it was set up," explained Rosen.[4]

One misperception was that if employees essentially "owned" the company, then they would be in control. Not so. No matter how you sliced it, Zell was both pilot and crew. "When we researched the companies where employees did have more control rights, we didn't find that the decisions that they made at the corporate level were significantly different," said Rosen. "So there's this perception that if the employees are on the board that they would run things differently. Well, the economic circumstances probably are more important in dictating what kinds of decisions get made. Changes at that level are not the cure-all that some people think they are. In this case it would probably be symbolically important. It's doubtful it would change anything in terms of how the company was run. But it might create greater transparency and a sense that people at that level are willing to listen to employee concerns."

On structural grounds, at least, Rosen essentially affirmed Zell's control over the ESOP, stating, "Contrary to what most of the stories say, the employees didn't invest their own money in this transaction. They got a stake in the company and their benefit plans would end up being in theory slightly to much better if this thing worked out even reasonably well. Should they get something when they haven't put any equity in directly, which Zell did, in terms of governance rights? That's a tough question. Most ESOPs don't."

But Rosen saw tremendous upside in changing the company's former management style so that employees have greater influence on decisions about how their jobs are done. "That's what really makes ESOPs more or less effective, and it's a lot harder to do that than to stick an employee or two on the board of directors and call it good. That really is the challenge that the Tribune or any ESOP company faces. As far as I know, the Tribune hasn't taken the steps to do that kind of comprehensive day-to-day involvement, and I think had they done that, they would be better off. Our research shows that makes the difference."

TRYING TIMES

It took more than eight months to close the Tribune deal, but why? Some pundits speculated that Zell got cold feet and tried to back out in the summer after Tribune's financial health slid closer and closer to the intensive-care ward. Revenue from classified and real estate advertising was dropping like a rock in early 2007 and showed little sign of ending its downward spiral as the months passed. Tribune revenues continued to nose-dive through the summer and into the fall of 2007. There seemed no end to the sour results.

Plus, there was the little matter of the bankers. They were getting nervous. Four of America's largest financial institutions— JPMorgan Chase & Co., Merrill Lynch, Citigroup, and Bank of America Corp.—backed Zell's Tribune deal but were beginning to fear that the huge debt load would ultimately doom the company. Collectively, during the delay in closing, the banks would see some $500 million in losses on the loans and high-yield bonds needed to fund the transaction. But once again, Zell's reputation won the day. "We believe in this transaction because we believe in Sam Zell," said James B. Lee Jr., JPMorgan's vice chairman.[5]

Another stumbling block to the sale involved Zell's all-time favorite partner of choice, the U.S. government. Tribune asked the Federal Communications Commission to waive its cross-ownership rule forbidding any company from owning both a television station and a daily newspaper in the same major market. Tribune had been granted temporary waivers for cross-ownership in New York, Los Angeles, Hartford, and South Florida. In Chicago, where Tribune

NEWSPAPER NEOPHYTE ■ 107

owned both WGN-TV and the *Chicago Tribune*, the FCC had issued a permanent waiver of the rules.

By mid-October, Zell and his team were getting antsy. They needed approval soon to close the Tribune deal before year's end. That approval came on November 30 in a sharply divided FCC vote.

The day of the closing, as agreed, Tribune CEO Denis FitzSimons announced his resignation, effective January 1, 2008. According to SEC filings, he also walked away with a tidy $38 million golden parachute in combined severance and stock after twenty-five years with the company.

Inevitably, questions immediately arose about Zell's focus and engagement with his new media empire. After all, he had a number of enterprises to run. "I think that's the 4,812th time in the last twenty years that someone has posed that exact question to me," Zell responded when questioned. "Each time I look at them and say, I don't know the answer to your question other than history says that Sam pays enough attention to everything Sam does, and Sam surrounds himself with a lot of very high-quality people with a lot of authority, and I don't think you'll find very many examples of any businesses Sam has touched that can claim that we ignored them or claim they didn't get enough of Sam's time. I think the same will be true here."

Zell installed himself as CEO but promised not to retain the mantle forever, saying he preferred to be an owner who could make decisions and cut through the notorious Tribune red tape. "I think the definition of CEO as you have historically known it has changed since yesterday (deal closing). Maybe I'm asking the $64,000 question, if the company even needs a CEO. We're going to find out. The answer is, I'm sure not going to be a conventional CEO. At the same time, I am one hundred percent accessible, and I'm going to do whatever it takes to achieve the objectives. Do I have enough time? Yep. Do I have enough ambition? Yep. Do I have enough determination? Yep. So you don't have to worry about that one.[6]

Zell would quickly find that the layers of dissent among Tribune's employees ran deeper than he anticipated, and the complexity of the situation would drain every last ounce of his management skills.

10

PAPER TIGER

AS THE LEADER of the third-largest media organization in the United States, Zell was uniquely in charge of either (a) building upon the very foundation on which the business of news would be built or (b) decapitating the beast and starting from scratch. Zell is a self-described "dispassionate" investor, one who admittedly understands history but is focused on the future and, in particular, future cash flows. He is rabidly deal driven, hates to lose at anything, and is expert at extracting the maximum value out of any given situation—as measured by bottom-line profits.

"The bottom line is that what happened in the past stays in the past," he said. "My head only looks forward, it doesn't turn backward. There is a lot of shit in the history of the *L.A. Times*, and I'm really sorry that I can't do anything about it. All I can do is address the future."[1]

Given some of his initial incendiary comments, journalists were rightly concerned to know exactly where their new change-agent leader might be taking them and their way of life. Most had never heard of him, but they did get a sense that this billionaire deal maker would be personally involved in their business. They burned through countless gigabytes of Internet bandwidth doing Google searches on Zell. What they found was a mixed bag.

Aside from the obvious deals he had won and lost, there was little to gauge his personal style. When it came to putting his money where his mouth was with philanthropic endeavors, for example, by the standards of modern-day billionaires, it turns out that Zell was only a modest giver. An avowed Zionist committed to the state of Israel, Zell does open his wallet freely to a variety of Jewish causes. He launched the Zell Entrepreneurship Program at the Interdisciplinary Center in Herzliya, Israel, north of Tel Aviv, in 2002. The program gives outstanding undergraduate students an inside look at advanced entrepreneurial studies in the creation of real-world business ventures.

Closer to home, Spertus College in Chicago created the Bernard and Rochelle Zell Holocaust Memorial, the first permanent Holocaust exhibition to be built in North America since 1975. It has become an important resource for local teachers and students, and the centerpiece of the Bernard and Rochelle Zell Center for Holocaust Studies. A Jewish day school in suburban Chicago, funded by Zell, also bears his father's name.

After his Tribune takeover, Jewish media couldn't get enough of him. Zell was described by the American *Jewish Daily Forward* newspaper as a Billionaire Boychik, *boychik* being Yiddish for "young man." This was a not-so-subtle reference to his buying one of the largest companies in an industry long known for its Anglo-Saxon heritage.

On occasion, both the *Chicago Tribune* and the *L.A. Times* had angered local Jewish community leaders with what they felt were negative stereotypes and anti-Israeli stances.

"The [*Chicago Tribune*] has a reputation for having a thick glass ceiling for Jews," said Michael Siegel, who for twenty-five years has been the rabbi at Chicago's Anshe Emet Synagogue, where Zell is a member. "For someone like Sam Zell, who is noted as a grave dancer, here he is more of a grave spinner. There are probably some past owners and executives who are spinning in their graves right now."[2]

But despite the causes and the kudos, many industry analysts and journalists feared that Zell was taking on an industry and establishment he could never fully understand or appreciate. More damaging was the very real possibility that his F-bomb style would never mesh with the hard-fought values of more than a century of journalism history. "Newspapers have historically been monopolies insulated from reality. I'm going to deliver a dose of reality," Zell boasted.[3]

Not unexpectedly, the message went down more like a poison pill. "When he was making the purchase, the media industry's response was 'What arrogance that he thinks he can come in and figure this out even though we couldn't,'" said Lauren Rich Fine, a thirty-year veteran media-industry analyst formerly with Merrill Lynch and then research director at ContentNext in Cleveland. "That's the response I kept hearing, that he doesn't know anything about media, so why does he think he can do it?"[4]

Fine, however, viewed Zell as more a breath of fresh air in an industry that had grown decidedly stagnant. "There are a lot of colorful personalities, but few and far between in the last ten to twenty years. Then you bring in someone like Zell, who has more personality than three people combined. It's not necessarily his crudeness or anything else, it's his willingness to just tell it like he sees it. I had been a very big proponent that when a model is broken, the best thing that can happen is to bring in an outsider who isn't shackled by the way things were but is a smart business person who can look at all the assets they have and see what they can make out of it. There was a fear because he's known as a cost cutter and a no-BS sort of guy and the industry has really tried hard to preserve the status quo. Insiders really don't want the business to change," said Fine.[5]

JOURNALISM'S DEEP ROOTS

When Walter Williams founded the nation's first journalism school in 1908 on the campus of the University of Missouri in Columbia, about halfway between St. Louis and Kansas City and only thirty miles north of the state capitol in Jefferson City, his basic premise was to create a centerpiece that would teach the profession of journalism.

Strolling across the verdant lawn of the Francis Quadrangle, the three-acre heart of the university's campus, six ghost-white marble columns are all that's left of the first academic hall after a fire destroyed the rest of the structure in 1892. These eerie guardians have become the university's enduring nod to both the past and the future.

All of the buildings situated around the Quadrangle are old-style redbrick structures, modeled after Thomas Jefferson's capitol and dome at the University of Virginia. Here also sits Jefferson's tombstone, donated by his heirs as a tribute to the university's pioneer status as the first built within Jefferson's Louisiana Purchase.

The newest resident of this historic district is strikingly similar—redbrick facade and all—tucked away in a cranny to the side of the quad. But behind the retro exterior sits a sleek and modern $30 million symbol of journalism's past, present, and future. The dedication of the new 47,000-square-foot Reynolds Journalism Institute in September 2008 paid homage to journalism school founder Walter Williams and came at a time when one of the nation's oldest institutions, the American newspaper, sits at a critical crossroads, perhaps even on the precipice of extinction.

Walking through the large wooden doors, visitors are met with sweeping vistas of airy glass and steel. Some might argue that this structure mirrors the state of today's newspaper industry—the wrapper may look the same, but what's inside needs to be different, even modern, and most of all, relevant.

During the three-day celebration of the journalism school's centenary and the inception of the institute, journalists from across the globe descended on Columbia to share their views on the state of the profession. One of the hottest topics of conversation was the future of newspapers and Zell's role in it.

THE "ELITE" MEDIA

Journalism as a profession is one of the hardest to quantify, and many critics complain of its lack of accountability. But for the past hundred years, writers and editors have followed one steadfast rule—it is their civic duty to get the story, inform the public, and be the people's eyes and ears.

Many of today's journalism schools crank out graduates who have practical, hands-on training in real-world media. As Walter Williams put it, "The best way to learn about journalism and advertising is to practice them."

Williams is perhaps best known in the profession for creating "The Journalist's Creed," a statement of journalism and advertising professionalism cherished as the most important pronouncement of its kind. Adorning the walls of the National Press Club in Washington, D.C., at its heart is a simple statement:

> I believe that advertising, news and editorial columns should alike serve the best interests of readers; that a single standard of helpful truth and cleanness should prevail for

all; that the supreme test of good journalism is the measure of its public service.

How much of Williams's ideals survive today is a contentious topic,
in media circles anyway. Certainly performing the "public service"
role is increasingly challenging, given the precarious economic condition of America's newspaper industry.

"Zell represents the most recent if not the strongest example of a
businessman who sees newspapers as a business. Period," said Dean
Mills, dean of the University of Missouri School of Journalism. "I
don't see Zell or any of these people as big villains. They are just
businessmen and they are approaching it as a business, which probably is inevitable at some point."[6]

As a former journalism practitioner as well as professor, Mills
quickly cuts to the chase when it comes to the foibles and future of
modern newspapers. "There was a golden age of metro newspapers,
probably from the 1960s to the 1970s, when newspapers were making money hand over fist and so were able to indulge their journalistic fantasies of great journalism. I think that age is over because one
of the main changes that new technologies have brought about is a
slivering of the audiences."

Mills continued, "There is this myth about the golden age being
a time when all the citizens got the newspaper on their doorstep
and learned what was going on at city hall and read it voraciously. In
fact we have readership studies going back to the 1930s and 1940s,
which show quite clearly that most people did not read what was
going on at city hall or the state capitol or whatever. Most people
bought the newspapers because they wanted one or two parts of it,
like the sports page or the crossword puzzle or whatever. It was this
great omnibus product, so what was really happening all that time
was the crossword nuts and sports nuts and the comics fans were

first thing he did was put a URL at the top of the newspaper," Zell remarked after the meeting. "That made a lot of sense, so I came home and I picked up a *Tribune* and I noticed our URL wasn't on the front page. A week later it was."[7]

Initially Zell settled into his comfort zone to find the right day-to-day chieftain for Tribune. He tapped top lieutenant Randy Michaels for the job. Michaels was transferred from his role as vice president and CEO of Tribune's interactive and broadcast divisions to the expanded role of chief operating officer, also in charge of the publishing unit.

Zell also knew that he and his fledgling team didn't have all of the answers. The day the Tribune deal closed, he announced a new online inbox, talktosam@tribune.com, dedicated to opening the communication channels with staffers.

"The first step toward increasing revenue and increasing profitability is increasing communication and increasing the flow of ideas, and at the same time creating a sense of urgency so that when somebody comes up with an idea, it doesn't get buried," said Zell. "We've got to have a company [where people talk] to each other and a company that really is a meritocracy where we really recognize achievement and we encourage achievement. What we've learned over the last seven months is there are a lot of really talented people in this company. We've got to change the way the company functions so we can extract from those people what they have to offer and give them the satisfaction of being serious contributors."[8]

Zell also used what he considered one of his primary assets in dealing with any new acquisition—the road show. He believed that his employees should get to know their leader, and he wanted to reinforce the fact that he would be anything but a typical corporate chieftain. To help jump-start his entry into the media business, Zell embarked on an initial coast-to-coast tour, meeting Tribune employees in every major market—Los Angeles, New York, Orlando, Baltimore, and Washington, D.C.

Early on, Zell showed signs of liberating Tribuners from some of their perceived shackles of the past. In particular, the news staff had expressed their frustration over having their Internet access filtered to block Web sites that might contain pornography. Zell was so incensed at this censorship that he had the blocks removed and let everyone know his decision via unfiltered corporate e-mail.

His whirlwind tour of visits to newsrooms and press facilities was choreographed to present Zell at his "I'm here to be your new leader" best. After all, this had worked with his other companies, where the sell had gone well. But Zell's message was blunt and to the point—the company had to turn around its fortunes, fast, and it needed all hands on deck to make that happen. This time around, however, the audience was different. It was dominated by a news crew, full of reporters who did not appreciate his calls for them to produce a product that would "sell" readers and viewers.

Thanks to the interactive age, Zell's colorful speeches were delivered in real time to millions around the globe via YouTube and countless blogging sites. Now a larger audience could make its own snapshot assessment of the man who dared to call for reporters to become more accountable to their audiences.

To be clear, Zell was not talking about a need for massive layoffs to help meet Tribune's enormous debt payments. Not yet, anyway. In fact, rather than make willy-nilly changes simply for the sake of change and to show that he was shaking things up, he wanted time to assess the situation, particularly the company's cash flow. Two days after the Tribune deal closed, Zell noted:

"It's really simple. If in effect your focus is just cost cutting, it's only a question of time before it's over, because then you get to the last person or last cost, and you have nothing left. It's not a direction for the future. That's not a direction for growth. I would tell you that I think we will have more employees a year from now than we have today. It's also unlikely that all of the deck chairs will all be in the same place. We didn't come here to go down on the *Titanic*. We came here to own the Empire State Building."[9]

Obviously, by this time, Tribuners were getting a better sense of their new owner. Another exchange between Zell and several *Chicago Tribune* reporters at a get-together in 2007 spoke volumes about the man. Asked why he bought Tribune Co., Zell remarked, "Because nobody has ever done it before. The true test of an entre-preneur is someone who spends his life constantly testing his limits. The definition of an idiot is someone who has reached his goals."[10]

SAM'S MEA CULPA

The Zell road show continued in early February 2008, as he made highly publicized stops at the *Los Angeles Times* and the *Orlando Sentinel*. Particularly memorable was a verbal exchange between Zell and *Sentinel* photographer Sara Fajardo, which quickly became the stuff of YouTube legend. At the end of Zell's final answer to Fajardo's question, he uttered, "Fuck you." Because the camera was focused only on Zell, it was not apparent what Fajardo had done to elicit the response—Zell says she turned her back on him before he was finished with his answer.

According to Zell spokesperson Terry Holt, he was offended by Fajardo's tone, not her questions. Holt noted that Zell had tried to reach Fajardo over the following weekend to apologize "if he offended her in any way." Fajardo left the paper several months later to become the communications officer for Latin America and the Caribbean at Catholic Relief Services in Washington, D.C.

The perception in media newsrooms from coast to coast was

quick and sure—Zell was not only autocratic and crass, but the new boss was truly out of control. At times, it seems that Zell knows, or at least acknowledges, when he has personally crossed the some-times invisible line between deprecation and demagogue. In one e-mail he explained that his raw language was deliberately intended to direct attention to Tribune's financial plight and the need for con-tinued cultural change. But he also issued a "mea culpa" to anyone who thought he had gone a bit too far.

Soon after what became known simply as the mea culpa, *L.A. Times* editor John Arthur expounded on Zell's comments with his own brief note to the editorial staff. In it, he downplayed Zell's remarks and reminded his minions that they should not follow his example when it came to the use of colorful speech in the newsroom.

Impersonal e-mails did little to quell the internal contagion that spread to the next stop on his road-show tour. In a town hall–style meeting with employees in Tribune's cavernous Campbell Hall auditorium on the seventh floor of Tribune Tower, Zell again clearly made the sense of economic urgency known, in equally colorful language. In essence, it was a "damn the words" moment:

AUDIENCE QUESTION: A number of people at the company, especially women, have been deeply offended by some of the statements you said in other places and other venues. I know you did the mea culpa, and I think we all know the history, but I wondered if you would address that here, because it's taken so long for people, and again especially women, to arise in the profession, and then they have felt personally disre-spected by some of your comments.

ZELL: First of all, I would not take back anything that I have said. I wouldn't take it back not because I disrespect women. As a matter of fact, if you look at my history, I have promoted more women to senior executive positions in my career than almost anybody else I know about. My number-one person for many years was a woman, an extraordinarily competent woman. So I don't have any issues of that at all.

But you turn it around and you put yourself in my position. You look at a company that requires fourteen signatures for somebody to go to the bathroom. You look at a company that requires ten signatures for somebody in York, Pennsylvania, to buy a ten-thousand-dollar Jeep. You listen to people in the newsroom at another paper than this one literally talk about their total disregard to the company, to the Tribune, that it's all about how do I win a Pulitzer Prize and I don't really give a shit about anything else.

You hear attitudes that we don't do it that way. No, we can't do that. Over and over again. I've got nineteen thousand people out there; some are men, some are women, some are other, I don't care. The challenge for me is how do I get your attention? Call me a schmuck, that's fine; call me disrespectful of somebody, prove it. I don't think anything I've said anywhere was directed at anything more than . . . this company lives without the eleventh commandment. And goddamn it all, we better get that eleventh commandment back on the front page here.

The eleventh commandment is, Thou shalt not take oneself seriously. Nobody is more self-deprecating than I am. If I can get everybody in this room to be self-deprecating instead of worrying about what's politically correct or what's not and instead worrying about How do we win? How do we succeed? How do we put out a better product? How do we make more revenue? How do we make a profit? How do we provide for our retirement? Those are the challenges. Pick on me on those issues all day long, but the real question for me is, How do I get your attention?

How do I get into a sense of urgency? How do I get you to understand that the future of this company is currently right out there in front of us, and if we keep operating the way we've been operating in the past, there is no future. OK? Plain and simple.

So you tell me, how do I get everybody's attention? Do I say, "Please? Hi, I'm here and I'm here to make all nice to you? We're not going to reduce any employment, we're just going to keep losing money." And then one day it's going to be over. So how do I get your attention?

I wrote that mea culpa, and I said I went over the line, and I went over the line on purpose, not accidentally. I went over the line on purpose to see if I could bring you to the edge. That's what we've got to do. I've got to get you to the edge. I've got to get you worried more about our revenue tomorrow morning than anything else. Because that's our survival.

Everybody's made this thing into this giant thing, OK? The L.A. *Times* has written about it, and they took it off their Web site. I told them to put it back on. Do you want me to talk slower?

How soon is this organization in this company going to wake up to the fact that we're on the edge, and we're either going to win or lose, and we better goddamn focus our efforts on how we get better, not on who's insulted. Nobody's trying to insult you.

I want to win, and I'm going to win. And what I'm looking for are the people in this company who are prepared to step up and not worry about this fuckin' thing or that fuckin' thing, but to worry about one thing—How the fuck do we win? And how do we get better at it, how do we generate more revenue, how do we make a difference? Those are the challenges, and along the way, how do we create an enormously successful corporation that provides both opportunity and sustenance for employees today and a future for them tomorrow.

That's the challenge. That's what everybody should be talking about. Not my fucking language, because it doesn't matter. And if it does, you're in the wrong place. And I'm not trying to insult anybody, I'm trying to get your attention. I'm trying to get you to understand this is the game, and we're either going to win it or we're going to lose it. If we spend an awful lot of time writing and pontificating about Sam's language, we're going to lose. If we spend a lot of time trying to figure out how we're going to generate more revenue tomorrow morning, then we're going to win. So that's my priority, and if that's not an apology, too fuckin' bad, I'm telling it to you straight.

I'm not disrespecting anybody, I'm trying to make everybody uncomfortable. I'm trying to put you in a position where it ain't so easy, it isn't like it was before, because that's the only way we've got a chance. If everybody gets quiet and settled down and comfortable like you were last year . . . this company lost $50 million of cash flow last year, and you never would have known it if you talked to anyone around here. Nobody knew it. Nobody cared. This business has been eroding before your eyes and you're worried about my language? Why aren't you worried about your customers, for chrissakes? My language ain't going to make any difference. I really am sorry if there's somebody offended, but nothing I've said was with that intent. Everything I've said was with an intent to get everybody to get off their ass and understand this is a crisis. We've got to save this business, we gotta make it work. And we've got to prioritize what we get all pushed out of shape about.

The history of this company is to divert from the reality. The reality is revenue is going like *this*, so let's focus on Sam's language, not on the fact that we're going right down the elevator shaft. Now how many articles did you read last week about my language and how many did you read about the reduction in revenue in the newspaper business? I rest my case.

Anybody else have any easy questions?[11]

QUANTITY VS. QUALITY

In his typically blunt and direct fashion, Zell was hitting hot buttons and taking dramatic steps to ask the kinds of tough questions that the media world had avoided for years—like how much are journalists worth and how do you measure their "performance"? Is it the prized "Pulitzer count" or some other metric? Or should it even be measured?

After months of internal meetings with Zell debating how to tackle the topic, Randy Michaels described the analytical process from a nuts-and-bolts business perspective in a conference call with Tribune investors in June 2008. Essentially, Zell and Michaels looked at Tribune's numbers and found the best way to trim costs was to create a newspaper model that basically yielded 50 percent advertising and 50 percent editorial content. Given the historical page count for Tribune's newspapers, that meant Zell and Michaels found they could shave five hundred editorial pages a week.

While an advertising/content balance of 60/40 or 50/50 was fairly commonplace in the magazine world, it was certainly an "out of the box" idea in newspaperland. And yet, there you had it, a cost-efficient idea for producing "newspapers of the future." Cut the bloody content.

On the call, Michaels went on to defend the stance, comparing the new model to a typical *Wall Street Journal* and noting that a skinnier *Los Angeles Times*, for example, would still be larger than the notable standard bearer of daily business.

But the pièce de résistance of Michaels's comments hit most journalists like a shot between the eyes. "We've also done something that I guess is new, which is that we've looked at the productivity of our journalists. We obviously look at the productivity of our sales-people, but nobody has ever said, how many column inches does a journalist write."

It turns out there are some really good reasons for that. For example, it takes longer to produce an investigative story than it does an obituary. According to Michaels, Tribune did some digging of its own, and the average journalist in Los Angeles produced about fifty-one pages of copy a year, while the average journalist in Hartford or Baltimore produced more than three hundred pages a year.

"I understand that there are different, extenuating circumstances and factors that have to be taken into account," said Michaels. "But we believe we can save a lot of money and not lose a lot of productivity. And so all I would say is if you work hard and you're producing a lot of output for us, everything is great. But we think we have a way to right-size the paper and significantly reduce our costs."[12]

Needless to say, this repudiation of the age-old culture that had become ingrained in professional journalism hit the rawest of nerves in newsrooms around the globe. This was sacrosanct territory, hallowed ground, even, and Zell was trampling all over it. But did he care what journalists thought of his "right-sizing" the business? Not one whit, especially if it meant buying time to shore up Tribune's eroding bottom line.

MR. CHANGE AGENT

Closely tied to column inches and page counts, Zell and his team embarked on an intensive program to redesign Tribune's newspapers in hopes of giving them fresh appeal to readers and, more important, advertisers. Leading that charge would be another of Zell's early and unconventional change agents, fifty-five-year-old Lee Abrams.

As Tribune's new chief innovations officer, Abrams certainly brought a colorful history to his role, and one that had little to do with the print medium. Abrams's main claim to fame was a ten-year stint as senior vice president and chief creative officer at XM Satellite Radio, overseeing the development and programming of more than a hundred radio stations. He developed programming for a star-studded roster, including musical artists Bob Dylan, Snoop Dogg, Quincy Jones, Willie Nelson, and Wynton Marsalis. Tribune journalists took notice—there was nary a Pulitzer Prize to be found in Abrams's background.

Prior to XM, Abrams was the founding partner of Atlanta-based Burkhart/Abrams and was widely credited with inventing album rock, the first successful FM format. He pioneered the radio "morning show" and gave Howard Stern and Steve Dahl their first major-market jobs. Abrams has also been a marketing and content consultant to MTV, Swatch, and Coca-Cola.

"Lee is the most formidable creative thinker in the media business today," Randy Michaels said in announcing Abrams's new role. "He invented the modern FM radio format, got satellite radio off the ground when no one gave it a chance, and managed to advise on the redesign of *Rolling Stone* magazine and the launch of TNT Cable Network in his spare time. Lee's going to pump new life into our content, reenergize our brands, and get people thinking and working together like they never have before."[13]

Abrams became known to Tribuners as less of a creative genius and more for his long-winded and often rambling "stream-of-conscience" e-mails. Like Zell, he polarized the place. To some he was a neophyte outsider who stood little hope of success in reinvigorating Tribune's print brands. To others he was a much-needed breath of fresh air to an otherwise stale industry that once viewed changing a masthead as an act of heresy to the journalism Gods. Only time would tell if Abrams would have the impact Zell desired. Expectations were high. After all, his boss was a man who loved to push the envelope.

11

NONCONFORMIST

RANDY MICHAELS AND Lee Abrams were two of the most visible cogs in Tribune's wheel, and they were emblematic of Zell's nonconformist style. They were outgoing, they easily embraced change, and they were decidedly anti–status quo. Zell's own leadership mantra demands that the contrarians around him also share his deep-seated sense of humor to go along with their thick skins. Take, for example, his "eleventh commandment," which, like the man, is pretty straightforward:

Thou shalt *not* take oneself seriously.

He mentions it often, especially in speeches that sometimes more closely resemble sermons. Those are words he lives by.

Zell is prone to public displays of self-deprecation and spends an unusual amount of time crafting zingers that poke fun not only at others but at himself as well. His idea of a practical joke, and his sense of humor, was fully exposed in a press release e-mailed to

Tribune staff on April 1, 2008—an important national holiday for any nonconformist at heart:

Tribune Company Announces Name Change

Zell Tells Employees of Switch in an Email;
Company Announces Revenue Generating Efforts To Offset Debt

CHICAGO, April 1, 2008—Tribune Company, the largest employee-owned media company in the nation, today announced it has changed its name to ZellCoMediaEnterprises Inc. or ZCMEINC. Zell, who made a fortune in real estate before deciding he'd like to dabble in an industry completely unfamiliar to him, announced the change in his record-setting 437th e-mail to exhausted employees this year.

"Hell, I put three hundred fifteen million dollars into this thing, and we're on the hook for thirteen billion—the least I ought to get is my name on the company's stationery," said Zell, who remains chairman and CEO of the newly named enterprise.

The company also announced a series of revenue-generating efforts, including a newly signed $600 million deal to rename historic Tribune Tower in Chicago. The new name of the landmark building will be unveiled at a ceremony held outside its Michigan Avenue entrance at noon today. Zell is expected to attend.

"While everyone was wringing their hands and worrying about renaming Wrigley Field, I went out and got a great company to put its product's name right over the main entrance to this great building," said Zell. "Finally we'll have the money to renovate the place and put in a heating and cooling system that doesn't date back to the days of Colonel McCormick."

Just to remind employees of how important it is that the company increase revenue in order to meet its considerable debt payments, the company has installed debt-o-meters at each of its business units and on the company website, www.tribune.com.

The company, which publishes nine daily newspapers in some of the country's top markets, also unveiled plans to go completely paperless, using edible ink and a newly designed licorice printing system.

"Now our newspapers can be put to good use for something other than news, information, and lining bird cages," said Randy Michaels, executive vice president of the company's broadcasting and internet divisions, who's also fooling around with newspapers. "Although I'm told it's a little dry, a family of four will be able to get a week's worth of nourishment off the Sunday edition of the Chicago Tribune."

Additional revenue-generating initiatives can be found on the company's website, www.tribune.com.

ZCMEINC (formerly Tribune) is America's largest employee-owned media company, operating businesses in publishing, interactive and broadcasting. In publishing, Tribune's leading daily newspapers include the Los Angeles Times, Chicago Tribune, Newsday (Long Island, N.Y.), The Sun (Baltimore), South Florida Sun-Sentinel, Orlando Sentinel and Hartford Courant. The company's broadcasting group operates 23 television stations, Superstation WGN on national cable, Chicago's WGN-AM and the Chicago Cubs baseball team. Popular news and information websites complement Tribune's print and broadcast properties and extend the company's nationwide audience. The company is also becoming known for its sense of humor and for not taking itself or its business too seriously. We suggest you check out the company website, www.tribune.com, for further proof of that.

Please note the date of this press release: Happy April Fool's Day.

MEDIA CONTACT:
Gary Weitman
VP/Propaganda and Disinformation
312/222-3394 (My office, where else would I be?)
gweitman@tribune.com[1]

Obviously Zell is no shrinking violet when it comes to taking on his critics, or himself, in equal measure.

UNCONVENTIONAL WISDOM

On a bitterly cold night in downtown Chicago after the Tribune deal closed, Zell was ready to head home after a long day of meeting and greeting. As he walked past the lobby's security desk, the guard startled him. He asked Zell if he had to wear a suit the next day, knowing Zell preferred casual garb and sensing an opportunity to dress down under the regime change. Zell's response, "I don't care what you wear, I only care about what you do. Nonconformity is wonderful."

That exchange speaks volumes about how Zell approaches life, both professionally and personally. "One of the great pablums of the world we live in is 'conventional wisdom.' My experience has been that conventional wisdom leads to conventional, predictable, and rather unexciting results. One of the things that I have always done is not accept conventional wisdom."[2]

Alignment with Zell's own nonconformist ideology is richly rewarded, especially when it comes to those who demonstrate ingenuity and creativity. At Tribune, his experience with former Jacor Communications lieutenants garnered them some of the company's top-flight management positions, primarily because he knew them to be problem solvers and Tribune had plenty of problems to be solved, in a hurry.

Zell's choice for Tribune chief operating officer, Gerald Spector, was a familiar face. Spector had joined Zell's growing organization in 1971 as an accountant, but was quickly put in charge of all of Zell's private companies for a time. Spector had spent the last fourteen years as the COO of Zell's Equity Residential apartment company.

"I asked Gerry to retire a year early to come over and help me with the Tribune, and he graciously accepted before he knew what he got himself in for, and now I don't take his phone calls," Zell laughed. "But the bottom line is Gerry is someone I have great respect and confidence in. He understands and has done this all before. It's really a focus on how do we become as efficient and effective as possible, how do we get things down to one person making a decision instead of fourteen? That's the world Gerry lives in."[3]

Surely there were a few out-of-work publishing professionals who could have been called back into duty to run the place? Absolutely. But to Zell that would be akin to more of the same, and that would be totally unbefitting of a change agent's modus operandi.

Even the makeup of Tribune's retooled board of directors raised eyebrows, dominated as it was by broadcast executives instead of traditional publishing and media experts. "The reason this board was put together is based on a bunch of people who think outside the box, who will challenge me, who hopefully know a lot more about a lot of things than I do. I never thought about them as radio people or TV people," said Zell. "These are creative, aggressive people who want to win. And they're all pissed because they think the newspaper business isn't dead and it ought to be relevant and it ought to work."[4]

As if to drive his point home, Zell is often quick to summarize situations in black and white, "let's just get on with it" terms. "There's a lot here to do and there's a lot here to achieve," said Zell. "And we're going to get it done. What we're looking for are twenty thousand partners who are in the boat with us and who are motivated, interested, and devoted to this objective. We are, and we're a lot like a bull in a china shop. We really plan on getting this done, and we're going to take along everybody with us who wants to play, and we're probably going to run over those who resist change. Change is what it's all about, and change is basically the definition of our future."[5]

That proclivity for change translated to reward for "out of the box" ideas. Zell was particularly taken by the concept behind Tribune's *Redeye*, a free weekly paper distributed to Chicago subway riders. "I looked at *Redeye* and I was riding my motorcycle to work one day and I was thinking about what made it work. You're delivering something to a very specific audience and you're making it edgy and colorful and interesting and you're getting people involved. If you get on the commuter trains right now everybody has got a *Redeye,* and that's awesome. I can't tell you how terrific that is.

"So the next question is what else can we learn from this?" Zell wondered aloud. "I started thinking wouldn't it be incredible to do the same thing in schools. You've got the same demographic, they all go to one place, so you don't have to have circulation other than to the place, they all have unlimited disposable income, they're a very hard target to get to, and so I called up and said, 'Gee, why don't subsidizing those of us who had this public affairs fetish and subsidizing reporters giving them the time to do the big projects."

To Mills, change is inevitable. "In terms of looking at what we do now, we just have to face it, that's over, and how are we going to do good journalism and invent the new models that will make it happen? It's just very hard to see how the daily metro newspapers are going to go on. We're already beginning to see about going to fewer days a week with print and emphasizing Web content."

And newspapers are not the only medium to see change. "The same thing is already beginning to hit local television stations," said Mills. "You're going to see a number of cities where the number of television stations will really come down to one or two in each market because the only reason they are going to have to exist is local news coverage, because nobody needs a tower anymore to distribute the entertainment stuff. It's the television model of the omnibus newspaper, where *I Love Lucy* supported Walter Cronkite."

TENSE TIMES INDEED

Amazingly, Zell's view of journalists is roughly the same as Mills's, but as an avid news consumer, he disagrees that newspapers are dead. And with Tribune, he had the world's largest media laboratory, with major resources and assets in the print, broadcast, and online mediums to find the right formula that works. What he didn't have was much time.

Even before the Tribune deal closed, Zell was talking with rival publishers to get a better idea of the lay of the media landscape. Early on, Zell visited with Brian Tierney, the CEO of Philadelphia Media Holdings, which owns the *Philadelphia Inquirer,* the *Philadelphia Daily News,* and the Web site Philly.com. "He said the we do that?' And they said, 'Well we studied it in 2002.' Does that sound familiar to anybody? But they studied it and didn't do it."

In typical Zell style, he openly marveled at the false start. But he was even more surprised when Tribune president Scott Smith strode into Zell's office the next day and threw a copy of a free newspaper called *TeenLink* on his desk. "It's exactly what I was talking about," said Zell. "It's designed for the high school kids, half of the content is written by the high school students. It was initially sponsored by a cell phone company and a group of junior colleges all desperate to target this market. And I said 'Holy shit, that's exactly what I want. Who does this?' And what did he say to me? 'We do.' In Fort Lauderdale, Florida, we are making money by producing a free weekly teen newspaper, and no one in this company knew about it.

"Think about what I'm saying," Zell chided. "We have a tower to share best practices. We have a successful effort and it doesn't come through? Literally nobody else knew about it. That doesn't make sense. That means how many other ideas are out there in the boondocks or in this building. That's the challenge. It's all there. We have extraordinary brands, we've got terrific people, and we've got very unique locations. We just have to figure out how to make them profitable and use them."[6]

People with simple yet creative ideas who then follow through on their implementation are the doers who get Zell's attention. One example is his choice of Tony Hunter as the publisher, president, and CEO of the Chicago Tribune Media Group. While Hunter was a fourteen-year veteran Tribuner, he was anything but the stereotypical publishing type. Instead, he was the senior vice president of circulation, a job he had held for only a year. He obviously made a large impression when he helped finalize a groundbreaking distribution deal with crosstown newspaper rival the *Chicago Sun-Times*.

As Tribune COO Randy Michaels put it, "It seems like Tony's been associated with the *Chicago Tribune* since Joseph Medill was trying to convince Lincoln to run for president. The important thing is that Tony has spent his life in the publishing business and we still think he's the right guy for the job. He understands the Trib and appreciates its history, but he's also a change agent, a creative leader who is eager to move the paper in a new direction so it can compete for more readers and advertisers."[7]

Obviously there are those who are less than charitable when it comes to Zell's change-agent mentality. Not content with daily tell-all blogs and insider diatribes of their own, in September 2008, current and former journalists from the *Los Angeles Times* tried jump-starting some change of their own through legal action. They named Zell and other Tribune managers in a class-action lawsuit filed in federal court in California.

Zell's response was swift and not unexpected, as he dispatched a press release:

> The lawsuit filed yesterday is filled with frivolous and unfounded allegations, and I hope every partner in this company is as outraged as I am at having to spend the time and money required to defend ourselves against it. The media industry is in crisis, the advertising environment is extremely difficult and the economy is in turmoil. The overwhelming majority of our employees have taken up the challenge—they are working hard, leading by example, and devoting themselves to re-inventing our businesses by developing new and innovative products for our readers, viewers and advertisers. As a company we are attacking our problems and revolutionizing the media industry.
>
> This lawsuit is a mere distraction, and we will work quickly to see that it is dismissed. It will not deter us from completing the work ahead.[8]

In what appeared to be a long-running war of words, the plaintiffs fired back their own stinging broadside:

> Zell's comments fail to acknowledge the billions of dollars in debt he caused the Tribune Company to incur, necessitating both the layoffs and the diminishing content of the Company's newspapers. It is unfortunate that, in typical fashion, Sam Zell is ignoring the rights and neglecting the best interests of the hard-working Tribune employees, whom he cynically refers to as "partners." Rather than working with his "partners," he is tearing the company down, brick by brick, and selling it off, in an effort to pay down the massive debt he improperly encumbered the company with. We look forward to cutting through Zell's self-serving, out of touch rhetoric and fighting for our clients—the Tribune's real and rightful owners—in court.[9]

This all made for great theater, but it had the earmarks of a long run. Ultimately it could take years and millions of dollars in legal fees before some resolution is achieved.

GOOD-TIMIN' SAM

In a never-ending attempt to live up to his own "unconventional" credo, Zell likes to set his own and decidedly spirit-filled agenda. "I'm a guy who has an extraordinarily good time. I'm a guy who really focuses on not being anywhere I don't want to be. And not doing anything I don't want to do," said Zell.

That sounds like a luxury for most working-class stiffs, but Zell never likes to party alone—he has such a good time that he openly and often encourages others to partake. Remember his eleventh commandment (Thou shalt not take oneself seriously)? Zell made it the virtual foundation of Tribune's policy manual and employee handbook, which he completely retooled shortly after his acquisition.

The free and loose language of Tribune's employee policies did little to quell some of Zell's harshest critics. Chief among them were many women in the media who were generally taken aback by his abrasive demeanor and off-putting lack of corporate decorum. But on this score—the issue of sexism—Zell's actual track record appears remarkably solid.

For many years, Sheli Rosenberg was Zell's right hand and top lieutenant. As director of Zell's holding company, Equity Group Investments, Rosenberg was in charge of the whole show from 1994 until she retired in 2000. In all, she was one of Zell's most trusted advisors for more than fifteen years.

Today, Rosenberg is one of the most accomplished women in Corporate America. She sits on the boards of major companies, including Avis Budget Group Inc., CVS Corporation, Cendant Corporation, Equity LifeStyle Properties Inc., Equity Residential, Equity Office Properties Trust, Nanosphere, and Ventas Inc. She cofounded and serves as president of the new Kellogg Center for Executive Women at Northwestern University's Kellogg School of Management. *Crain's Chicago Business* even named her one of the "100 Most Influential Persons" in Chicago.

More recently, Zell promoted women to top positions at Tribune. For his beloved *RedEye* free daily newspaper, he tapped Tran Ha to oversee its editorial content as well as that of *The Mash*, a weekly paper for Chicago public high schoolers she launched in 2008. At the same time, he promoted former *RedEye* cofounder and editor Jane Hirt into the managing editor slot of the *Chicago Tribune*, the second most powerful position at the paper.

POLITICAL PERSUASION

Given Zell's ties to big business and close proximity to the Chicago political scene, many media watchers worried about his potential influence on the editorial policies of his many newspapers. When it comes to editorial matters, he has made it clear that he would not try to foist his own views and beliefs on his newsrooms. "Do I look naive enough to think I have any influence about what people write?" he asked a group of Tribune reporters the day he bought the company. "In fact, I will accept that your writing on me is going to be, hard to believe, worse than it has been."

Still, Zell couldn't resist cracking the door open to interpretation on his view that the business of news is closely intertwined with the actual content that appears in the newspaper pages. "If you are relevant, people are going to buy the newspaper. If you're not relevant, then people will stop buying the newspaper and stop advertising and we'll all be in a stew of trouble. I use that word 'relevant' and I'll be the first to tell you I don't know what it means other than, in effect, ultimately just like anybody, you have customers, and some way or another we have to find a way how to service them. I don't have an opinion as to what you write, believe it or not, other than what you write has to be truthful and relevant. And if it is, then I think the customer is there for you, and that translates into viable businesses."

If the 2008 U.S. presidential election was any barometer, editorial independence has a strong chance of survival. Both the *Chicago Tribune* and the *L.A. Times* formally endorsed Barack Obama for president. For the *Tribune*, the endorsement was a milestone, as it was the first time in the paper's history it supported a Democratic presidential candidate. Of course, it didn't hurt that Obama happened to be from the land of Lincoln, Zell's beloved Illinois.

Zell often puts his money where his mouth is when it comes to championing all things Chicago. His hometown won Zell's support in July 2008, when he contributed $100,000 to Chicago's bid to host the 2016 Summer Olympic Games. During the 2008 U.S. election campaign season, he contributed far more to state and federal Republican candidates ($76,400) than to Democratic candidates ($10,200). Zell openly wears his probusiness, antigovernment sentiment on his sleeve, but has been known to disparage both Democratic and Republican politicians if they espouse policy positions that run counter to his own.

ATOP HIS SOAPBOX

No matter what the subject, Zell has a viewpoint that he is more than willing to share with those who will listen. His speaking schedule has him constantly in motion. Packed crowds of business students, corporate leaders, and entrepreneurs alike are all hungry to hear whatever tiny kernel of knowledge they might glean to help them become the next Sam-like billionaire entrepreneur.

His friend Peter Linneman recounts a favorite Zell classroom moment during one of his frequent visits to the Wharton School of Business. "He did my entrepreneurship class, and then it came time for the question-and-answer period. One of the kids said, 'I think you're really great and I admire you and all that you've done and I want to be just like you in five years.' Sam looked at him and said, 'Why the hell do you get to be like me in five years when it took me forty?'

"I always found that to be the most profound statement he made, because while he made it tongue-in-cheek, he also made it very seriously," said Linneman. "The point was not becoming him; it was

[that] becoming whoever you are going to be is an ongoing process and that professional success is not crafted in five years, it's crafted in a lifetime. It's a fundamental, off-the-cuff insight. It is also representative of Sam in a fundamental way. He has a great way of understanding some basic truisms and yet putting them in a context that has a sense of humor and yet a sense of deep earnestness."[10]

POMP AND CIRCUMSTANCE

To supplement the speeches and college visitations, early every summer, Zell begins thinking about his annual year-end "gift" to friends and colleagues. Since 1976, he has commissioned the creation of an original music box complete with a catchy song that speaks to some important aspect of the financial markets. For an entrepreneur like Zell, gifts of fruit and chocolate somehow seemed to lack originality. He preferred to make a more memorable personal statement.

One recent New Year's box, adorned with a bronzed man holding an umbrella, featured an original Zell-produced video complete with a song based on the onetime B. J. Thomas classic "Raindrops Keep Falling on My Head":

> Capital is raining on my head—
> Everything is liquid, we're awash with cash to spend
> The flood has drowned returns
> 'Cause assets keep liquifying, monetizing, raining . . .

Birthdays for Zell have taken on a cause célèbre tone as well, giving him a chance to lavish up to a million dollars on the pomp and circumstance. On this score, he has taken a page directly from the scrapbook of former media mogul Malcolm Forbes, who was known for throwing lavish affairs in rather unique venues.

Zell is careful to create a top-secret Chicago location for the hundreds of guests he invites each year. Past parties have featured themes such as "Arabian Nights" at locales as diverse as the Aragon Ballroom, the Cirque du Soleil tent, a barge taking guests to a decorated abandoned factory on the city's North Side, and boats departing the Navy Pier to sail underneath the Chicago Skyway.

Weeks in advance of the shindig, invited guests receive a specially designed T-shirt matching the party theme. Mirroring the man himself and his love of all things casual, the shirt must be incorporated into some aspect of the guest's attire to gain admittance to the festivities. In 1999, while the Y2K phenomenon was beginning to preoccupy many people, Zell's tongue-in-cheek shirt read "Z2K" and "Zellenium."

For Zell's sixty-seventh birthday in 2008, invitees were sent T-shirts matching the "One Enchanted Evening" theme. Some eight hundred guests were bused to a remote abandoned shipyard outside the city that was converted into a tented fantasyland complete with live performers, a carousel, and endless food and drinks.

Guests, who included former Tribune combatant Ron Burkle and former Playboy president Christie Hefner, also received a card with a clue to identify the night's entertainment. That year it happened to be the Eagles. Prior shindigs featured performances by James Brown, Elton John, Little Richard, Bette Midler, and Aretha Franklin. One year Jay Leno literally rode a motorcycle into Zell's gig inside the Marché restaurant in downtown Chicago.

"I was fortunate enough to be invited to two of his birthday parties, and those are always quite something," said Jonathan Kempner. "They had the largest shrimp I've ever seen in my life, flown in from Madagascar. They were the size of lobsters."[11]

ZELL'S ANGELS

Zell the risk taker shares something else in common with the patriarch of corporate cool, Malcolm Forbes—he is a motorcycle aficionado, a recreational love affair that started when he was a student at the University of Michigan.

Forbes pioneered the concept of the carefree corporate chieftain, and his true passion was motorcycling, which he embraced in the late 1960s. In the 1970s and 1980s, Forbes formed a riding group of Wall Street hotshots and fellow CEOs known as the Capitalist Tools. Largely due to his highly publicized international motorcycle trips with Hollywood celebrities, business leaders, and the press, Forbes helped change the general public's perception of what motorcyclists and motorcycling were all about. He showed that motorcycling was not only socially acceptable behavior, but even a highly desirable pastime for people of all social walks.

Zell's own riding club, dubbed Zell's Angels, is known for tearing up roads from Eastern Europe to South America to Italy for a week every summer. "That's the week I spend in my helmet, by myself."[12] How seriously devoted is he to this guilty pleasure? He once missed a Tribune board meeting to ride with his buds in Switzerland.

While much is made of Zell's need for speed, what many observers see as risk taking, Zell actually views as cathartic and motivating. He often mentions how many ideas his free-riding generates. Several days a week, he has plenty of time to conjure on the long ride from his Highland Park home into downtown Chicago.

Zell has also used his enthusiasm for motorcycles for charitable causes. In 1998, the Zell's Angels made a fifty-person appearance at a gala he hosted to open the Chicago segment of the Guggenheim Museum's touring show "The Art of the Motorcycle" at the Field

Museum of Natural History. Zell underwrote the exhibit's Chicago stay, and the whole affair was typical of his against-the-grain style. The show was a radical departure for a history museum, but it was designed to attract new audiences from local and regional markets to the venue, particularly hard-core bikers and those "weekend warrior" riders who enjoy biking as a lifestyle element.

Fearing a possible media backlash for holding such a radically different show, the museum hired a public relations agency to coordinate the event. It included a Biker Ball opening-night fund-raiser and a made-for-media Saturday morning seven-mile ride led by Zell and museum president John McCarter. The ride was such an event that the City of Chicago shut down Lake Shore Drive for a time. The museum broke new ground thanks to Zell's involvement, helping to identify it as more than your father's tired old history museum.

Zell's nonconformist ways even extend to his motorcycle of choice, an Italian Ducati. Aerodynamically sleek and oh-so-chic, the Ducati brand is pure speed and motion, a rolling piece of sculpture on two wheels. Instead of a steel frame, it uses lightweight aluminum to save weight and improve handling. The company, founded by three brothers in 1926 in Bologna, even became a target of Zell's takeover prowess when he offered to pay 300 billion lire for a 50 percent stake in the company in 1995. That offer was later rejected in favor of a more lucrative bid of $320 million from an American investment fund.

Bikes will continue to be part of Zell's trademark, if for no other reason than that their mystique offers him a chance to continually reinforce his own uniqueness. After visiting the corporate offices of Tribune Co. to size up his new prize, he cheekily remarked that his bright yellow Ducati would fit nicely in the cavernous wood-paneled office of the company's former legendary CEO, Colonel McCormick.

Zell's risk taking extends to the ski slopes. Many a colleague can recount the indelible image of Zell's tiny form, clad in a bright yellow jumpsuit, bouncing down a black-diamond run, poles flailing at his sides.

"We used to have this conference up in Aspen, and Sam's a great skier," said Stan Ross of the USC Lusk Center for Real Estate. "He asked this twenty-year-old guy if he wanted to race down the mountain. The kid looked at Sam and thought, here's an old guy, he could take him. He puts on his helmet and his skis, and Sam doesn't put on a helmet, and down the hill they go. This kid comes down the mountain and gets to the bottom figuring he won, but there is Sam sitting at a table with a bottle of champagne. That's the legend, anyway."[13]

12

REVOLT

TO SAY THAT Zell's legendary nonconformist ways were not easily accepted in the world of big media would be an understatement. For those trying to get a true reading of the man, the real book on Sam Zell is one of polarization. There are those who admire his raw, unvarnished temperament and business success, and those who see him as a modern-day pirate, complete with a sailor's lexicon.

The latter opinion was starkly displayed early on, in public, shortly after Zell took over Tribune. Zell ordered a new banner hung in the lobby of the *Los Angeles Times*, reading "You own this place!" He thought it would be well received as a rallying call to the troops. He was wrong. The next day, a group of *Times* employees hung a huge placard down one side of the *Times* parking garage reading "ZELL HELL Take back the *Los Angeles Times*." Now that's loyalty for you.

While Zell knows how to roll with the punches, at times, it seemed that the constant jabs and criticism hit his rawest nerve. "You think I need to do this?" he snarled in a town hall–style meeting with Tribune employees back in Chicago. "You think I needed to take on the Tribune because this is my way to maybe get a plane, or maybe I can live in a penthouse, or maybe I can have a house in California if this works? I got all that shit, OK? So I'm out here busting my ass and I'm swearing at you and you and you and everybody, and I'm saying get the fuck up and realize that this is it, man. This is our chance. And we either make it or we don't make it. And I can pussyfoot about it, I could tell you nice little stories and we can all go off into the sunset and down the elevator shaft loving all the vignettes. But you know what? At the bottom of the elevator shaft, they have this special room called 'politically correct.'"[1]

Zell's unconventional methods of communicating with Tribuners won him countless detractors as the early weeks of his regime change rolled across the company like a Midwestern F5 tornado. One telling example became a daily reminder for all Chicago-based employees at the Tribune Tower headquarters. Zell, a fan of Oregon modern artist Michael Speaker, installed a statue of a harried businessman adorned with eighteen legs and six briefcases in the ground floor lobby. It came to publicly symbolize Zell's distaste for all things red tape and wanton decision making.

"I thought maybe it would catch your attention," said Zell. "But what is it saying? Here's this guy and he's running around in place, he's got eighteen legs and six briefcases and he ain't getting nothing done other than creating process. We can make our organization flatter, more responsive, capable of making decisions faster, responding to environment, eliminating bureaucracy."[2]

Zell quickly decentralized decades of budgeting and accountability, pushing those functions away from the Tribune Tower and down to frontline managers. Shortly after taking over, Zell recounted a conversation with the publisher of the *L.A. Times*. "I had breakfast with David Hiller this morning, and basically what I said to him is I'm expecting him to be president, CEO, and publisher of a business called the *L.A. Times*. To the extent there are benefits that come from collective purchasing, maybe collective sale of ads and various other things, he will benefit from that. But in the end, he and his team have got to be responsible for the *L.A. Times* and responsible for the P&L of the *L.A. Times*."[3]

Hiller's New Year's resolution list included firing *L.A. Times* editor James O'Shea, the former *Chicago Tribune* editor who'd relocated to his Los Angeles post little more than a year earlier. To say the dismissal did not go over well would be an understatement. Zell would soon come to see firsthand the deep-seated resentment that the *L.A. Times* staff held for his cost-cutting measures and nearly any other move that emanated from Chicago.

O'Shea's outgoing (and lengthy) diatribe to his fellow journalists spoke volumes about the pent-up animosity toward Zell and Tribune management in general. In certain passages, he made it plain that the manifesto was his going-away present to both the *L.A. Times* newsroom and to Tribune management.

Not surprisingly, Zell's reaction to O'Shea's missive was swift and terse, but O'Shea's ousting was just the beginning of a larger wave of staff reductions brought on by what Zell described as a deeper slump in advertising revenue than anticipated. As Zell promised, within sixty days of closing the Tribune purchase, the formal cuts began on February 13.

Zell reiterated his "we will not achieve success by just cutting costs" stance, but the reality was that Tribune was not making enough money and something—people—had to give.

Zell was cutting staff positions in the publishing group and corporate office through a combination of voluntary separation, involuntary layoffs, attrition, and closing open positions. His goal was twofold—cut costs while flattening the organization's structure to foster nimbler decision making.

In Los Angeles, in the midst of the cutting, the one position Hiller couldn't live without was an editor, and he had that gaping editorial hole to fill. Newspaper editors have traditionally earned their stripes via Pulitzer Prizes or breaking big investigative stories in Washington, D.C. But on Valentine's Day, Hiller quickly tapped Russ Stanton as the paper's new editor. Stanton was a ten-year *L.A. Times* veteran and the leader in turning around the paper's LATimes.com Web site. He was the paper's fourteenth editor and fourth in less than three years.

Though lacking the traditional reporting pedigree, Stanton's experience in the online realm was a deciding factor in his promotion. But more changes, i.e., staff cuts, were on the way. Throughout the summer of 2008, the deep staff cuts kept coming as Zell and Michaels took every opportunity to trim what they viewed as unnecessary layers of management and resources that were impeding decision making. July 14, 2008, was quickly dubbed Black Monday. Early in the day, Hiller announced his resignation as publisher of the *L.A. Times* in a slightly more gracious note than O'Shea's.

While it would be easy and expedient to say the cuts were deepest with Tribune's West Coast problem child, hours later the contagion had spread eastward, as veteran *Chicago Tribune* editor Ann Marie Lipinski resigned. In an e-mail to the paper's staff, she never directly addressed her reasons for leaving, but the timing was more than coincidental.

FORCED TO ACT

By the end of the bloody summer of 2008, staff cuts had been deeper than originally anticipated. Tribune had chopped more than a thousand jobs across the company's newsrooms, mostly at the *Los Angeles Times*, and Zell seemed to have contradicted a few earlier statements about cost-cutting measures.

Asked if he was as optimistic in June 2008 as he was just six months earlier, Zell opened his kimono a bit. "When we bought the company, we believed that the future of the newspaper was going to have to be different than it had been in the past. We underwrote the investment on the thesis that we would have a period of time to make the transition. As everybody knows, advertising revenues in the newspaper industry have drastically dropped, particularly classified advertising as it's moved to the Web. The result is we have been forced to act much quicker and take what we had originally envisioned as our 2010 plan and implement it in 2008," said Zell. "I still believe there is a good future for the newspaper business. There is a need to recognize that the role of the newspaper has dramatically changed in the last twenty-five years. Our goal is to define what role a newspaper can have in the future and to produce a newspaper that economically justifies its existence."[4]

Media analyst Lauren Rich Fine wished Zell had done more to shake things up. "We did know we were at the edge of a cliff, we just didn't know how high," said Fine. "It was not a well-timed purchase; it dragged on longer than he might have liked. He probably himself will come out OK. But the biggest surprise to me is that he didn't come out shooting faster. He had a lot of time to look at this, and given that he's trying to break the cultural barriers anyway, I don't know why he didn't move even faster. He was going to get criticized for what he did, so he might as well have gone faster."[5]

Long-time confidante Peter Linneman summed up Zell's predicament best. "He is running a race with the capital markets and the economy, and the trend is moving against him. If he can get his fundamentals from the operating side improved fast enough, he will survive, but he's got to do it faster than he originally planned, and that's going to be a challenge that everybody in the business has got."[6]

WELCOME TO MOGULVILLE

Once upon a time, owning a newspaper was akin to owning the crown jewels, only more valuable. Thomas Jefferson noted their importance back in 1787, saying, "Were it left to me to decide whether we should have a government without newspapers, or newspapers without a government, I should not hesitate a moment to prefer the latter."

Whether willingly or not, Sam Zell joined a cast of media moguls who have graced and disgraced newspapers around the globe for decades. He is certainly not the first larger-than-life personality to stir the ranks of journalists. Who can forget the likes of flamboyant British investor Robert Maxwell, who bought up the *New York Post* as his virtual plaything, then thanks to hubris and greed lost it all, including his own life, in a mysterious yachting accident.

Despite his self-professed sales bravado, Zell values his privacy and his roots, and he is anything but the stereotypical media mogul. He doesn't live in New York, preferring the broad-shouldered streets of his familiar Chicago. He does own the perquisite corporate jet, in which he logs some 1,200 hours annually, but in business he flies decidedly under the media radar.

Before Zell's takeover of Tribune Co., the dominant media figure in the United States was an Australian, Rupert Murdoch. Four years Zell's senior, Murdoch arrived in the United States in 1974 and has been squarely in the media's bright gaze ever since. Unlike Zell, Murdoch was schooled early in life as a journalist—his father ran the evening newspaper in Adelaide during his youth. An acknowledged conservative, Murdoch for decades has worried media critics who are concerned that he is more interested in harnessing the power of his media brood to further his own political and personal agendas.

Murdoch drew near-Zell-like ire after closing his own $5 billion purchase of Dow Jones & Co. in 2007. The great fear was that Murdoch would, in short order, dramatically transform the *Wall Street Journal*'s content in his own conservative political image. However, the worry appeared for naught, particularly since Murdoch was under certain constraints imposed by the paper's founding Bancroft family that helped insulate editorial functions from his direct influence. Zell, on the other hand, had potentially free rein to do as he pleased with his own editorial control over Tribune's media properties.

Prior to buying Tribune, Zell addressed potential media-control issues this way:

> Within the world of conspiratorial thinking, the obvious assumption is that I have some extraordinarily devious path and as soon as I get control, I'm going to turn the newsroom over to the elephants or I'm going to bring the American Conservative Union into the pressrooms. But the answer is, I have the self-confidence to believe that given the right structure, given the right kind of analysis, and given the right kind of management, we can succeed.[7]

In the final analysis, comparing the two might be akin to stacking a vintage Merlot up against a bottle of Ripple. "I don't think Zell belongs in the sentence with Murdoch yet," said Fine. "Rupert Murdoch is the guy to watch right now. He bought Dow Jones for a fortune and had the same insight that it was going to be a challenging environment. And he keeps investing, and at the same time he's had some rough moves along the way, too. He grew up in the business and really understands what he's doing, but he's not awed by the way it used to be. I love watching his strategic moves, because he's thinking so far ahead of everybody else in terms of what he's going to create. I don't see that kind of vision coming from Sam Zell."[8]

VENDETTA?

To most journalists, Zell's vision was clearly muddied, not to mention hopelessly trapped in a time warp. "He just appears to be prosecuting old grudges and bringing old baggage to it, not creating a vision of what the future of newspapers would be," said Kevin Roderick with LA Observed. "Even before the layoffs, people were fleeing because they were seeing there are other media executives out there who have a clue of where things may be headed. Even with the *Wall Street Journal,* Murdoch is building for the future and is creating a path to future prosperity. Then they look at Zell, who didn't have a path to anything and was more about tearing things down."[9]

To Roderick and other Los Angeles journalists, Zell was on a mission all right—to get even. "In L.A., the view was that he was getting even, that he'd somehow drunk some Kool-Aid from dissidents within the Tribune culture in Chicago and was going to exact revenge in Los Angeles against journalists, whom he clearly doesn't like or respect. Everything that he signaled is that he doesn't view the *Los Angeles Times* as a major asset within journalism, as if they've been straying off the reservation and need to be brought back into the Chicago way of thinking about things. It was disappointing to most people," said Roderick.

There was also an unmistakable sense that Zell had only a single chance to win over his journalist partners, and he failed on numerous occasions, largely because he recognized but failed to fully comprehend the depth of skepticism inherent in the breed.

"Clearly he liked to be thought of as a cowboy and outside-the-box thinker and actor, and I guess he is," said Roderick. "I think it is an essential question to answer—how much of the style that he puts on is an act and how much is real? When he went to the newspapers and was cussing and then he came out and said that was all just an act, I didn't talk to one person who was there that believed him. They said it was not an act, it was flashes of anger. It was authentic anger, not leadership, not trying to change any culture. He's got some things that haunt him about journalists, and he was going to act on them."

13

FIRE SALE

WHILE ZELL IS not given to understatement, he does often produce simplistic analogies to describe his strategic thinking, even when it comes to the workings of multi-billion-dollar enterprises. "It's like we have a pile of Lego blocks on the table and we're going to, in effect, re-create this company in a kind of virtual fashion and by doing that we're going to see what works and what doesn't work."[1]

Throughout the Tribune bidding war, Zell repeatedly said he would focus first on communication and restructuring rather than deep cost cutting, agreeing only to sell off the Chicago Cubs and Wrigley Field. But even before the battle for Tribune was won, the company was disposed to dispose.

In March 2007, it sold two southern Connecticut newspapers, the *Stamford Advocate* and *Greenwich Time*, the smallest of Tribune's eleven papers, to Gannett Co. for $73 million. That deal was scrubbed just two months later after Gannett refused to assume the contracts of the union representing reporters and photographers.

Ultimately, privately held Hearst Corporation bought the two papers in October 2007 for the reduced price of $62.4 million.

Tribune also made a few strategic real estate plays in early 2008. First it sold its studio and production lot in Hollywood for $125 million, then its Southern Connecticut Newspapers real estate in Stamford and Greenwich for $30 million. It used the proceeds, plus $30 million in cash, to structure a so-called like-kind exchange to purchase property it was leasing from TMCT LLC in April 2008. The deal helped Tribune defer taxes on the earlier sales.

ZELL'S STILL GOTTA SELL

More sales were on the way. In early 2008, the wakeup call came when it was apparent that Zell's analysis of Tribune's financial travails was a bit wide of the mark. Advertising continued to slump, dragging down profits at the newspapers, cash he needed to help repay the bankers as debt obligations came due.

"Probably our toughest year is 2008," Zell remarked. "It's going to be a shitty year and we're going to have to do a whole bunch of things to make sure that we don't get hurt. Number one, it's manageable. Number two, I have a lot of experience running and managing highly leveraged institutions. And I don't think this is any different than any of them. I'm not a newspaper guy, I'm a businessman. Therefore all that matters in the end is the bottom line, because as long as we have a bottom line we have a viable newspaper. If we lose that bottom line or erode it significantly, then we're all going to get buried together. And that ain't a good deal."[2]

Soon the whispers in Zell's ears were growing louder, as potential suitors lined up outside his door to buy up various Tribune assets, particularly *Newsday*. The New York newspaper, a sixty-eight-year-old daily tabloid serving the city's Long Island and Queens residents, was among Tribune's most profitable properties, but a sale would certainly help Zell meet his first hefty debt payment of $650 million due in December 2008. And right on its heels, another $750 million debt bill was due in May 2009.

Zell and Rupert Murdoch, the Australian financier and fellow media mogul, had become better acquainted after Zell's protracted negotiations over Tribune. Murdoch had purchased Dow Jones and with it the *Wall Street Journal* in December 2007 for $5.16 billion from the Bancroft family in a protracted contest similar to that of Tribune and the Chandler clan. Murdoch had not formally entered the Tribune fray, fearing the debt levels he would assume, but he was keenly interested in partnering with Tribune to print the *Wall Street Journal* at Tribune printing plants, or at least create a joint venture between *Newsday* and the *New York Post* whereby the two entities would reduce costs by sharing content production.

There are few secrets in the publishing world, and when the prize is New York readers' hearts and minds, it did not take long for interest in *Newsday* to gather steam. Suddenly, three of New York's most powerful media moguls—Murdoch, Mortimer Zuckerman (a fellow real estate/media titan and owner of Boston Properties, a big office REIT, as well as *U.S. News & World Report* and the *New York Daily News*), and Cablevision chief James L. Dolan—showed a keen interest in tightening their grip on New York's lucrative media market.

Murdoch faced an uphill challenge in his bidding. Federal Communications Commission cross-ownership rules forbid one entity from owning two major media in any one market. Murdoch owned the *New York Post* and two television stations in New York. Zuckerman owned the *Daily News*. Only Murdoch would have to seek an FCC waiver on the ownership rules.

Initial interest in *Newsday* was lukewarm at best. What Zell needed was an auction to help extract the highest price. He created one by agreeing to a deal to sell to Murdoch for $580 million. That, in effect, created a floor for the auction, as Murdoch was unaware that two other bidders were knocking on Zell's door.

Zuckerman matched Murdoch's bid, secure in the knowledge that he would not have to beg the FCC for an ownership waiver. Then Cablevision leapfrogged them both, offering up $650 million. Murdoch, though, thought his deal would win the day and publicly at least, he was claiming the deal was struck. "I don't think Cablevision will prevail. Just be patient for a couple of days," Murdoch told investors on a conference call. "We're certainly not in the business of getting into an auction here," he said. "We're hoping to wrap it up within the next week. We think everything is in hand."[3]

But was Murdoch willing to bid higher, knowing it could negate the potential savings he sought in combining the *Post* and *Newsday* operations, as well as stir up angst among News Corp. shareholders who thought newspapers were already getting too pricey? Three days later, Murdoch suddenly withdrew his bid, and the Dolan family and Cablevision steered to the inside track. After all, they were willing to pay more money and agree to Zell's joint venture structure, something that would help Zell avoid a hefty capital gains tax bill. Cablevision, with its subscriber base of some 3 million strong, was also based on Long Island, *Newsday*'s home turf.

On May 12, 2008, Zell sold a 97 percent stake in Newsday Media Group to Cablevision for $650 million. Once again, he had drawn a Royal Flush to win yet another game of high-stakes poker with some of the world's top deal makers.

In the immediate aftermath, however, the sale raised more questions than it answered. After all, he seemed to be selling off one of his prime cash cows. What was Zell's strategy for Tribune's future? Would he invest in the company or sell other flagships, especially as they were less profitable than *Newsday*?

Zell repeatedly insisted he would not sell either of his remaining marquee newspapers, the *Chicago Tribune* or the *Los Angeles Times*. But that didn't mean some other properties wouldn't go on the auction block.

FOR SALE: TRIBUNE'S HOME

Because Zell is invariably described as a real estate maven, it came as no surprise to most Zell watchers when the first rumors began to swirl about a possible sale of Tribune's real estate assets, including the venerable Tribune Tower in Chicago and Times Mirror Square in downtown Los Angeles.

One of Zell's favorite quotes is from noted American architect Daniel Burnham, who famously said, "Make no little plans, they have no magic to stir men's blood and probably themselves will not be realized. Make big plans, aim high in hope and work."

Though born in New York, Burnham was raised in Chicago, and surveying the city's downtown skyline, it is easy to see what Burnham meant. Chicago is generally regarded as the home of American architecture. Masters of the iconic like Burnham were drawn to the Midwestern city thanks to the tragic fire that nearly leveled it in 1871. By 1909, Burnham would prove to be one of the city's leading lights thanks to his Plan for Chicago. The centerpiece of the plan was the creation of parks stretching all along the city's natural river and lake fronts.

Today, a myriad of glass-and-steel towers pay homage to great American architecture. And while the monolithic dark and brooding hulks of Sears Tower and the John Hancock Center dominate the view, one of the most enduring icons of the 1920s remains a fixture. Lit up at night like a limestone wedding cake, the Tribune Tower is the result of a design competition in 1922. The winning architects, John Mead Howells and Raymond Hood, received a $50,000 check for their neo-Gothic design, which featured a flourish of unique "flying buttresses" near the top of the tower.

Under the watchful eye of Colonel Robert McCormick, the Tribune Tower quickly became the past and present symbol for the modern American newspaper. Just to drive the point home, a statue of Nathan Hale, the American spy who was hanged by the British during the revolutionary war, stands as a solemn sentinel outside the tower's main entry. In 2006, the McCormick Tribune Freedom Museum, devoted to continued study of the First Amendment's impact on American freedom, was opened on the first floor.

History is often tinged with irony, as demonstrated by another classic building located just a few blocks away. It is hard not to notice that Zell's own base of operations, Equity Group Investments, is headquartered in the former Chicago Daily News building, an Art Deco structure made out of Indiana limestone and now known as 2 North Riverside Plaza, overlooking the Chicago River.

Zell and business partner Lurie bought the building back in 1976, when they were still just "real estate people," long before the notion of owning a Chicago landmark like the Tribune Company was even a glimmer on the horizon. Designed by noted Chicago architects Holabird and Root and built in 1929 on the doorstep of the Great Depression, the building is the first to be constructed over railroad tracks.

In a further twist of irony, the *Chicago Daily News*, an afternoon paper started in 1875, folded in 1978 after severe declines in circulation and advertising sales. Many pundits pointed to the rise in television viewership and the flight of core downtown readers to the suburbs as primary causes for the newspaper's demise. Today's newspaper industry is fighting a similar battle in an increasingly 24/7 world, not only from television, but more so from the Internet.

BATTER UP

Zell watchers well understood his disdain for emotional attachment to Tribune's legacy, and many feared he would take the same approach to yet another of Chicago's most vaunted institutions. One of his most watched moves was the sale of the 132-year-old Chicago Cubs and their landmark shrine to baseball's old-school roots, Wrigley Field. Rumors that the sale would happen surfaced in June 2007 when Tribune put itself on the auction block. Once Zell took over, he was required to sell them off because he already had an ownership stake in the crosstown rival Chicago White Sox.

Selling the Cubs and the stadium, though, proved to be a complicated mess at times. First there was the bureaucracy, a root concept that Zell openly detests. Major League Baseball franchise owners must submit requests to sell a league club to MLB commissioner Bud Selig. The league then approves the winning bidder, not always based on price but also on subjective factors including financial backing and operating experience. At least 75 percent of the other twenty-nine team owners then must vote in favor of a winner.

Certainly the Cubs were not just another baseball team. Throughout their storied history, they have long been known as the loveable losers, thanks to their unique ability to snatch defeat from the jaws of victory in oh-so-close title games.

That historical track record hasn't prevented the Cubs from becoming one of the richest teams in baseball, however. More than 3 million fans have crammed into the tight 41,160-seat Wrigley Field to see the Cubs play their home games from 2004 through 2008. And this is a team that had not even been to the World Series since 1945 (when Zell was just four years old) and had not won a championship in one hundred years.

To say Zell is a sports fanatic would be akin to a foul ball. In fact, he seemed to care less about the onfield gamesmanship than he did about the balance sheet, especially because the Cubs paid out more than $100 million a year in player salaries. "We own a baseball team that pays one guy $25 million a year to be right one out of three times," he quipped. "It's a business I don't understand, so I'm going to pass the risk on to somebody who either understands it or gets enough psychic income that they don't give a shit."[4]

But it is history and nostalgia that draws the fans to Wrigley Field by the legions. Built in 1914, Wrigley is the second-oldest ballpark in the major leagues behind Boston's Fenway Park, opened in 1912. The record books show that Wrigley was the historic site of Babe Ruth's famous "called shot" when Ruth pointed to the center field bleachers in game three of the 1932 World Series and promptly cracked a home run. And another Sammy, Sosa, hit his sixty home runs in 1998, 1999, and 2001 in home games at Wrigley Field.

In Chicago, Cubs fever runs deep through the community, and rarely has a sports franchise generated such passion among its fans. Not surprisingly, Chicagoans were up in arms over Zell's decidedly nonchalant approach to selling their beloved institutions. But what they didn't understand was that Zell is at his best when he can create a "buzz" around whatever he owns. The old adage that "There's no such thing as bad PR" is definitely a Zell maxim.

To jump-start his debt repayments, Zell was hoping for a quick sale of the team, the stadium, and Tribune's 25 percent stake in cable channel Comcast SportsNet by the season opener on March 31, 2008. But everything hinged on selling Wrigley Field first. He and Cubs chairman Crane Kenney took a potential deal to the Illinois Sports Facilities Authority (ISFA), which owns U.S. Cellular Field, the stadium where the crosstown Chicago White Sox play. The idea was to involve the quasi local/state agency, formed in 1987, to inject monies into renovating Wrigley Field.

Kenney's first priority was keeping the Cubs at Wrigley; thus the need to sew up the stadium deal first. "We all had hoped the stadium deal could move more quickly," Kenney told Major League Baseball. "We also understand that with all the legislative input needed, why it won't move as quickly as we hoped."[5]

It turned out the state had a lot to play for—Wrigley Field was the third most popular tourist destination in the state.

WHAT'S IN A NAME?

Throughout its storied history, the Wrigley family, of chewing gum fame, never paid a dime to have its name prominently associated with one of baseball's shrines, even after Tribune bought the team and stadium from the Wrigley family in 1981 for only $20.5 million.

Could it be that Zell would trample on that heritage? You bet. Naming rights are big business—Citicorp ponied up $20 million for the naming rights to the new New York Mets stadium in Queens. Once again, Zell showed his audacity in asking Wrigley to pay up, even though the firm does not directly market the stadium to sell its products. To Zell, this was another untapped revenue source. And again, he was asking the questions that few were willing to ask.

According to Kenney, that possibility, though viable, held third place on his top to-do list. "We want a championship, that's Goal 1," Kenney said after a management session at the 23rd annual Cubs Convention. "We also want a wonderful stadium to see that championship in. That's Goal [No.] 2. Goal [No.] 3 is what's the stadium's name. I put them in that order. If doing something differently with No. 3 allows us to have a championship in that ballpark, then we'll do it."[6]

Zell fueled the public debate over the sales process in February

2008. "Excuse me for being sarcastic, but the idea of a debate occurring over what I should do with my asset leaves me somewhat questioning the integrity of the debate. There are a lot of people who would like to buy the Cubs and would like to buy the Cubs under their terms and conditions and, unfortunately, have to deal with me."[7]

That juxtaposition could be seen in a physical sense as well. The Wrigley family's corporate home, the Wrigley Building, was built just across the street from Tribune Tower in downtown Chicago.

BREAKING UP IS HARD TO DO

Several potential bidders, though, had already balked at separating the two entities, believing that strategy diminished the value of both franchises. Also, the stadium itself needs extensive renovations to keep pace with basic needs—like clean restrooms and better food vendors—and that could weigh heavily on the stadium's price tag.

Former Illinois governor and ISFA Chairman James Thompson proposed spending $400 million on renovations, to be paid by selling individual seats at Wrigley—think the sporting version of a condominium. But Zell argued that the Internal Revenue Service and Major League Baseball would balk at the tax ramifications of that structure. By June 2008, the ISFA and Zell stopped talking altogether, and they never came back to the table.

Even before the ISFA deal fell through, Zell had quickly scrambled up the next logical path—warming up the bid group approved by MLB. Bid books were distributed to a group of ten suitors approved by MLB in mid-June 2008.

First-round bidders in July 2008 included Mark Cuban, the combustible and controversial owner of the National Basketball Association's Dallas Mavericks, the Chicago-based Ricketts family, which owned TD–Ameritrade Holding Corp., and an investment group called Sports Acquisition Holding Corp., which included former congressman Jack Kemp and former Atlanta Braves baseball great Hank Aaron.

Cuban's bid topped $1.3 billion, and if successful, anything in that league would have made the sale the most lucrative deal for an American sports team, exceeding the record 1999 purchase of the National Football League's Washington Redskins for $800 million, and the $700 million purchase in 2002 of the Boston Red Sox, Fenway Park, and the majority of a regional sports network. However, in November 2008, the Securities and Exchange Commission charged Cuban with insider trading violations. He pulled out of the Cubs bidding contest and sued the SEC in May 2009 to gain access to documents used in the SEC investigation. A Dallas judge dismissed the SEC charges against Cuban two months later.

Zell's timing of the Cubs sale was a decidedly mixed bag. In the fall of 2008, the team made it as far as the playoffs, then crashed and burned in a three-game shutout by the Los Angeles Dodgers, an ironic twist, considering Tribune's own internal/infernal newspaper feuds between Chicago and L.A. Unfortunately the worldwide financial markets also did some crashing of their own, at least temporarily stalling Zell's sale plans.

At one point it seemed almost nothing was sacred, as even the Wrigley's name was in flux. In September 2008, Wm. Wrigley Jr. Co. was sold to privately held Mars Inc. in a gargantuan $23 billion deal that effectively hit the delete button on one of Chicago's oldest companies and created the largest confectionary company in the world. The Wrigley's brand, gracing candy wrappers since 1923, and management may stick around, but there is no denying it's the end of yet another Chicago institution.

Miraculously, after a nearly two-year auction process, a winning bidder emerged, and it turned out he was a local made good. Chicago billionaire investment banker Tom Ricketts, son of TD Ameritrade discount stock brokerage founder J. Joe Ricketts, plunked down $845 million for the Cubs and Wrigley Field in August 2009.

After twenty-eight years of corporate ownership, the Cubs were back in the hands of a local family. And Zell achieved yet another notch in his legend—largest sale of a sports franchise in history—despite the naysayers and a badly burned economy.

PUMPING UP INTERACTIVE

Even as Zell was selling off assets, he and his management team were focused on maximizing internal operating efficiencies. It was classic Zell—streamline management and decision making to create a nimbler organization that could more quickly take advantage of new opportunities, whether homegrown or market driven.

He went on to drive the point home, always fearful that listeners aren't fully absorbing his message. "I want decision-making to happen quicker. I want information to flow faster. I want connectivity to exist and I have the sense, from the outside, that we haven't done a great job of that to date. Fixing that and improving that is going to have enormous implications across this company."[8]

While making significant cuts in the publishing operations, Zell was making good on an early promise to beef up Tribune's interactive division to enhance its editorial contributions.

Like Murdoch, Zell believed that some combination of print, broadcast, and Internet properties was the key to unlocking Tribune's true value. "We think that if anything that the history of this company is that there has not been enough cross-fertilization and there has not been enough cross selling and that that represents a significant opportunity going forward," said Zell.[9]

In September 2008, he appointed a new "content team" to both increase Internet search-engine optimization and develop new content across all of Tribune's online assets. The team included players from each of Tribune's major markets, including Los Angeles, Chicago, Orlando, and Hartford.

Zell and Michaels also recruited former broadcasting talent from Jacor to run the interactive group. Tribune Interactive President Marc Chase named Jana Gavin senior director/business development for Tribune Interactive. Gavin was part of a growing team of Jacor veterans now working for Tribune, which included Chase, Sean Compton (senior vice president/programming for Tribune Broadcasting), Steve Gable (chief technology officer), Russ Gilbert (vice president/digital innovation), and Special Consultant Roy Laughlin.

With another online property, CareerBuilder, Zell extracted $135 million in cash value by selling an additional 10 percent stake in the joint venture to Gannett Corp. By the end of 2008, Gannett held a majority 50.8 percent stake, while Tribune held 30.8 percent, the McClatchy Co. 14.4 percent, and Microsoft a 4 percent interest.

Ultimately it may take several years for Tribune's interactive work to pay off from a revenue standpoint, but some signs are at least encouraging. During the 2008 presidential election, both the *Los Angeles Times* and *Chicago Tribune* Web sites saw record activity in the number of users and page views.

KA-CHING

One of Zell's most important moves was naming Eddy Hartenstein, the founder of DirectTV, as the new *Los Angeles Times* publisher in August 2008. Hartenstein became the paper's fourth publisher since 2000 but was the first with Southern California roots to hold the job since Otis Chandler.

Cagey as always, Zell designed his recruitment of Hartenstein to stem the angst emanating from the West Coast crowd. Raised in Alhambra, California, Hartenstein began reading the L.A. Times at age eleven and expected his familiarity with the community and with the paper to be a major plus.

"To be publisher here in L.A., you need a local, and I am a local," he told an overflow crowd of Times employees at an afternoon meeting. "I'm a 213 kind of guy, not a 312 kind of guy," he quickly noted, referring to the area codes for downtown Los Angeles and Chicago, respectively. Hartenstein had the credentials to run a successful enterprise—albeit in the broadcast realm—and assured Times staffers that Zell had given him six months of unobstructed freedom to scout the local landscape and produce needed changes.[10]

While most of the headlines about Tribune's moves dealt with slashing costs and firing journalists, aka "cost centers," Zell's team was busy focusing on another logical function, the primary driver of revenue, sales. Here Zell felt most comfortable, for it was a subject near and dear to his heart (and his pocketbook).

One of Hartenstein's first moves was to group all Times advertising sales functions, including interactive, under one person. For this challenging role, he named veteran sales guru Scott McKibben as the Times's new executive vice president and chief revenue officer, which was a brand-new title there. McKibben had a long career in newspaper sales, once holding the title of president and publisher of San Francisco Examiner & Independent Newspaper Group and most recently with Freedom Communications, where he oversaw the Orange County Register.

The L.A. Times staff members might have welcomed one of their own, a local industry veteran, with open arms. Unfortunately, they didn't. Times journalists discovered that McKibben had sued the Fang family, the former owners of the San Francisco Examiner, for

$1.2 million in unpaid commissions he was allegedly due for bro-kering the sale of the paper and its parent company for $20 million to Denver billionaire Philip Anschutz. Shortly after the sale, McKibben went to work for Anschutz. The Fang family then sued Anschutz, but the suit was settled out of court.

Meanwhile, Zell was doing what he did best—piling the pressure on Tribune's sales staff to be top producers or be gone. "[Salespeople] ought to look at themselves in the mirror and ask themselves, 'Am I hungry? Do I want to make a lot more money and do I want to work a lot harder?'" said Zell. "If the answer to all those questions is 'yes,' they've got a great future. If they look in the mirror and say, 'Gee, I'm an order taker and I don't really want to work harder and I don't want to do anything,' then maybe the outlook is bleak. Because part of what we've got to do here is make this company aggressive. We've got to make everybody go for it. I'm going for it, shouldn't everybody else? And particularly a sales force, because in the end we live and die by revenue. And it's that sales force that we're depending on the revenue for."[11]

A PRODUCT OF THE TIMES

Unfortunately, revenue continued to be in shorter supply. Certainly this was a systemic problem for the newspaper industry, but it led to continued speculation that Zell's bet on Tribune was particularly ill timed. After all, the company's financials had been deteriorating rapidly for the past two years.

Proof positive of the state of newspaper advertising was all around Zell. In June 2008, McClatchy Newspapers announced 1,400 lay-offs as a result of lower advertising revenues after buying Knight Ridder. The theory was well founded in 2006—snatch up groups of

newspapers with loads of debt and create efficiencies to grow revenues across the board. In fact, McClatchy got off to a roaring start,
quickly selling off a dozen papers to help pay down some debt.

That strategy failed at precisely the moment the U.S. economy
faltered, particularly in California and Florida, where McClatchy
had its highest concentration of titles. After McClatchy took $3 bil-
lion in noncash goodwill impairment charges related mostly to those
papers in 2007, the $4.6 billion Knight Ridder deal looked consid-
erably less valuable. And $2.5 billion in debt was not going away,
making growth a huge challenge thanks to high debt and principal
payments.

Obviously one by-product of efficiency is often a reduced labor
pool. But in one case, Tribune came out on top of the jobs-lost equation for a change. When its *South Florida Sun-Sentinel* cut a deal to
print the *Palm Beach Post, Palm Beach Daily News,* and *La Palma,*
the papers' owner, Cox Newspapers, slashed three hundred employees as a result. Zell was not the only newspaper publisher desperate
to make ends meet, as others also understood that sometimes soldiers would have to be sacrificed to save the enterprise.

Mergers and consolidations of news-gathering operations, once
an unthinkable exercise that would dilute the intrinsic value of
"local" in local news, became a commonplace occurrence in the
latter months of 2008. Once again, Zell was leading the way by
example. Perhaps the most radical shift was his drastic decision to
fire half of Tribune's forty-eight-person bureau in Washington, D.C.,
in November.

By the end of 2008, more journalists were out of work than at
any time in history, as the U.S. Department of Labor estimated that
some twenty-one thousand newspaper industry jobs had been lost
over the past year. Tribune and its brethren were obviously swimming against the tide.

14

FAILURE *IS* AN OPTION

ALL OF THE fire sales, staff cuts, and pithy diatribes in the world couldn't help Zell or Tribune win their race against the astronomical debt payments coming due each month. The rumors of Tribune's demise swirled around the company for weeks before reaching wider media circles on Sunday, December 7, 2008.

Zell had been negotiating with his creditors through well-known workout consultants Lazard Ltd. and Sidley Austin. While Tribune had enough cash on hand to make a scheduled $70 million debt payment to junior bondholders on Monday, December 8, Zell faced a sort of D-day financial conundrum: Draw down much-needed cash to make the payment, continue hoping that advertising revenue would pick up, and sell the Cubs in time to make an even larger debt payment in June 2009—or not?

This time around, Zell's reputation was not enough to win the high-stakes game of chicken with his creditors. Billions were now at risk and the banks could ill afford to restructure their loans, given their own precarious financial footing. The financing terms would remain unchanged. So Zell blinked.

Tribune's bankruptcy became official on Monday, December 8, and with it, Zell added another first to his résumé—largest media bankruptcy in history, with the largest debt load. The filing was explained in a Tribune press release:

> CHICAGO, December 8, 2008—Tribune Company today announced that it is voluntarily restructuring its debt obligations under the protection of Chapter 11 of the U.S. Bankruptcy Code in the United States Bankruptcy Court for the District of Delaware. The company will continue to operate its media businesses during the restructuring, including publishing its newspapers and running its television stations and interactive properties without interruption, and has sufficient cash to do so. The Chicago Cubs franchise, including Wrigley Field, is not included in the Chapter 11 filing. Efforts to monetize the Cubs and its related assets will continue.[1]

He described Tribune's predicament as the result of "the perfect storm. A precipitous decline in revenue and a tough economy have coupled with a credit crisis, making it extremely difficult to support our debt." The bankruptcy filing would allow Tribune to restructure its heavy debt burden. "We believe that this restructuring will bring the level of our debt in line with current economic realities, and will take pressure off our operations, so we can continue to work toward our vision of creating a sustainable, cutting-edge media company that is valued by our readers, viewers and advertisers, and plays a vital role in the communities we serve. This restructuring focuses on our debt, not on our operations."

In an e-mail to Tribune staff, Zell also made it clear he was not abandoning the company in its time of need.

A review of Tribune's filing in Delaware revealed a decidedly lopsided balance sheet, with debts of $12.9 billion and assets of $7.6 billion. Tribune's largest senior creditor, JPMorgan Chase, the nation's second-largest bank after its timely takeover of the failed Washington Mutual, was owed $1 billion. Other senior creditors, including Deutsche Bank AG and investor Angelo Gordon & Co., were owed $737.5 million and $324.5 million, respectively.

Also in the filing, Tribune cut off payment of severance and deferred compensation, and also stopped payments to freelancers. Even former Tribune executives were left in the cold on their severance packages. Particularly hard hit was former Tribune CEO Mark Willes, who was owed $11.2 million in retirement and deferred compensation.

MEANT TO BE?

One could legitimately argue that it was all meant to be and in many ways preordained. Zell's near-pristine track record of prescient timing was bound to fall short at some point. From the beginning, there was a certain inevitability about the Tribune deal, a stacking of the cards against it. From the rancorous reception given to Tribune's new boss to the worst economic downturn since the Great Depression, this one had all of the earmarks of failure from day one.

For months he had known the diminishing dimensions of the tiny financial corner in which he had painted himself. Standard & Poor's had lowered Tribune's bond ratings to B from B+ as early as February 2008, and the company had hemorrhaged cash since he landed in the CEO's chair. So it is legitimate to ask why he did not choose the reorganization option a bit earlier. But to know Zell is to know boundless levels of optimism matched only by a deep recalcitrance when it comes to admitting his mistakes. He would be slow to admit that failure was, indeed, an option.

The final straw came as Zell was briefed on Tribune's third quarter 2008 financials. In early November 2008, Tribune reported a swing to a huge third-quarter loss of $124 million after making an $84 million profit for the period only a year earlier. Severance costs alone had mushroomed to $45 million in the quarter, versus $4 million the previous year. The tally across the publishing division was enormous—total advertising revenue was down 19 percent, national advertising revenue was down 21 percent, and classified was down 30 percent. Even the interactive division saw a 7 percent drop, and broadcasting and entertainment revenues slid by 6 percent. The company's debt was pegged at $11.4 billion.

Publicly, Zell knew he was sounding like a broken record on Tribune's quarterly conference calls. "We are operating in an exceptionally difficult financial and economic environment," he noted. "The newspaper industry continues to see extraordinary declines in ad revenues, and Tribune is no exception. But, we continue to aggressively pursue our operating strategy and to tightly manage the factors that are within our control. Internally, we have established momentum on developing new initiatives, and our culture now reflects that focus and mindset."

But he was finally, once and for all, tired of running the viability race. Not to mention the fact that his creditors' clarion calls of concern were growing louder. One of the key covenants in his deal with the banks as senior lenders was a figure known as the debt-to-earnings ratio, essentially the ratio of debt to a company's earnings before interest, taxes, depreciation, and amortization. If Tribune's debt became greater than nine times its cash flow, the company would be in technical violation of its loan covenants. You spell that D-E-F-A-U-L-T. Though Zell appeared to view the covenant as more of a nuisance that could be renegotiated given the realities of the banks' difficulties, it provided yet another reason to file Chapter 11.

Zell maintained that the Chicago Cubs were not included in the bankruptcy filing, and it was fortuitous that the sale of the baseball franchise and Wrigley Field had stalled until after the bankruptcy filing. If the sale had been completed on the original timetable, by the end of 2007 or the fall of 2008, considering the magnitude of the financial services crisis and the mounting losses by Main Street banks and Wall Street powerhouse firms alike, Tribune's creditors may well have demanded early debt payment rather than allow Zell to hoard the funds to reinvest in operations.

FALLING IN

An unusual story in the world of postmortems: Here is one of the smartest businesspeople around, and he got it horribly wrong. The gleeful grave dancer had fallen down a pitch-black hole with seemingly no bottom. Naturally there was a never-ending stream of "told you so's" and a lot of piling on. But the question still remained, how did this happen to Sam Zell?

Two days after the bankruptcy filing, he was in an uncharacteristically somber mood when he appeared in a CNBC interview with Maria Bartiromo. Asked point-blank what went wrong, Zell's response was deadpan and matter-of-fact.

> I think in the most simplistic terms, we looked at the Tribune before we made our offer. It had basically eroded at about a 3 percent level in the previous five years. We underwrote it at 6 percent and we ended up with 20 percent.

In an operating leveraged business like this, 20 percent reduction in gross revenue is a disaster on the cash-flow line. In the end, my response to it is to preserve the value of the company and to make sure that it will go on into the future. Our action was preemptive in nature so as to preserve the assets of the company and create the opportunity for reorganization. Had we had a 2007 or 2006 year, we would not have had any issues at the Tribune. But under the circumstances, it was like a giant tsunami or perfect storm. When you lose that kind of revenue, there is no way to overcome it.[2]

But didn't Zell bank his business career on predicting these sorts of tsunamis? Wasn't he the master of timing, riding the wave, unloading at the peak and avoiding the collapse? One argument is that he relied too closely on personal counselors who were not correctly attuned to either the ways of the media or the potential for a near-collapse of the worldwide financial system. After all, he had weathered perfect storms before.

THE POLITICAL MACHINE

Bankruptcy in business, which exacts an unmerciful toll on reputations and paychecks alike, can be overcome by more favorable economic breezes and the passage of time. The real problem, or rather temptation, comes when financial trouble attracts those who would exploit it—the equivalent of moral bankruptcy.

Most troubling in the days following the Chapter 11 filing, the hits just kept coming, as both Zell and Tribune were swept up in an ever-widening political scandal that threatened to further taint their legacies. Less than a day after Tribune's filing, agents with the Federal

Bureau of Investigation knocked on the door of Illinois Governor "Hot" Rod Blagojevich at six A.M. They immediately arrested the governor, still in his sweat suit, while across town, his chief of staff, John Harris, was facing a similar fate. Both were apprehended on federal corruption charges brought by U.S. Attorney Patrick Fitzgerald.

The arrest of a prominent politician and his chief of staff was a surprisingly brazen move, even in the rough and tumble world of Illinois politics and after an exhaustive five-year federal investigation into the governor's alleged wrongdoing. "I can tell you one thing, if Illinois is not the most corrupt state in the United States, it's certainly one hell of a competitor," noted Robert Grant of the FBI during a press conference.

While much of the initial discussion centered on an alleged plot by Blagojevich to sell the U.S. Senate seat for Illinois vacated by president-elect Barack Obama to the highest bidder, there was a tantalizing tidbit involving Tribune in the headline of the draft announcement:

> Blagojevich and aide allegedly conspired to sell U.S. Senate appointment, engaged in "pay-to-play" schemes and threatened to withhold state assistance to Tribune Company for Wrigley Field to induce purge of newspaper editorial writers.

As the impact of the events settled on media outlets across the country and the U.S. Justice Department's allegations became more widely known, Zell, Tribune, and Wrigley Field were tossed deeper into the smoldering cauldron, thanks to the public release of the seventy-eight-page criminal complaint, entitled "Misuse of State Funding to Induce Firing of *Chicago Tribune* Editorial Writers."

Essentially, the affidavit spelled out a scenario whereby in early November, Blagojevich directed Harris to speak to Tribune about its pending deal with the Illinois Finance Authority for the sale of Wrigley Field. The affidavit alleged that Harris told a Tribune associate, identified as "Tribune Financial Advisor," that state financial assistance would be withheld unless members of the *Chicago Tribune* editorial board, who Blagojevich thought were stirring up talk of his possible impeachment, were fired.

In a November 4 phone call, Blagojevich allegedly told Harris that he should say to Tribune Financial Advisor, Cubs Chairman and Tribune Owner, "our recommendation is fire all those [expletive] people, get 'em the [expletive] out of there and get us some editorial support."

According to the affidavit, Harris spoke with Tribune Financial Advisor on November 10. In an intercepted call a day later, "Harris allegedly told Blagojevich that Tribune Financial Advisor talked to Tribune Owner and Tribune Owner 'got the message and is very sensitive to the issue.' Harris told Blagojevich that according to Tribune Financial Advisor, there would be 'certain corporate reorganizations and budget cuts coming and, reading between the lines, he's going after that section.' Blagojevich allegedly responded, 'Oh. That's fantastic.' After further discussion, Blagojevich said, 'Wow. Okay, keep our fingers crossed. You're the man. Good job, John.'"

In the affidavit, Harris allegedly told Blagojevich that he had singled out Tribune's deputy editorial page editor, John McCormick, "as somebody who was the most biased and unfair."[3]

After the affidavit was made public, Tribune issued a quick but somewhat perfunctory press release on the matter. In part, it stated that ". . . the actions of the company, its executives and advisors working on the disposition of Wrigley Field have been appropriate at all times. No one working for the company or on its behalf has ever attempted to influence staffing decisions at the *Chicago Tribune* or any aspect of the newspaper's editorial coverage as a result of conversations with officials in the governor's administration."

Chicago Tribune editor Gerould Kern also added his two cents, stating, "No one within Tribune Company has ever complained to me about the positions taken by our editorial board, or attempted to influence our coverage of the governor in any way. It should be clear to anyone reading our recent coverage of the governor and his administration that it is fair, balanced and factual."

But this matter was far from being put to bed like so much yesterday's news. In fact, it drew comparisons to a recent case involving another major Chicago publisher. In July 2007, Conrad Black, the head of Hollinger International, owner of Tribune's crosstown rival, the *Chicago Sun-Times*, was sentenced to more than six years in prison after he was found guilty of mail and wire fraud and obstruction of justice. The lead U.S. attorney in that case? Patrick Fitzgerald.

With each passing day, the Blagojevich saga produced highly charged drama with ever-deepening layers of intrigue. The day after the governor's arrest, the identity of the Tribune Financial Advisor referenced in the complaint turned out to be none other than Nils Larsen, a Tribune executive vice president, managing director in Zell's Equity Group Investments and a close Zell confidante in charge of the Cubs sale. Larsen was named to *Crain's Chicago Business*'s "Forty Under Forty" list in 2007, and was already a twelve-year veteran of Zell's teachings. No charges of wrongdoing were leveled against Larsen.

For his part, Zell admitted he was being brought into the unfolding Blagojevich drama in a CNBC interview:

MARIA BARTIROMO: "Have you been contacted by the FBI, Sam?"

ZELL: "Uh, yes."

BARTIROMO: "And they're looking to see if there was any pressure, really, on the Tribune staff?"

ZELL: "I think they're asking questions. As far as my knowledge
   is concerned, the Tribune did not respond at all."
BARTIROMO: "And as far as you're concerned, was there pressure
   on the staffers to change coverage?"
ZELL: "I certainly can't speak to that."

The FBI subpoenaed Tribune correspondence regarding the allegations that the governor had tried to improperly influence Tribune's editorial coverage and staffing in exchange for an expedited purchase of Tribune's Wrigley Field. Ultimately no Tribune editorial writers were fired, and apparently Zell and his team stood firm in rebuffing Blagojevich's alleged requests. "If anyone tried to muscle the Tribune Company, they did not succeed," noted John McCormick, deputy editorial page editor for the *Chicago Tribune* and the primary target of Blagojevich's alleged wrath.[4]

IS THIS "THE END"?

The double whammy that struck Tribune will have an impact not only on the company's operational future but also on the reputations of Zell and those around him. Certainly his potential for profits was diminished with the bankruptcy filing, which gave creditors and the judiciary far more say in the company's future.

Zell's statements to journalists nearly a year earlier, when the hope for a turnaround of Tribune was so promising, proved prophetic. "Philosophically, this is a great challenge, it's a great opportunity. It's not going to change my lifestyle, no matter what happens. It's likely to change yours significantly. But it's not going to have any impact on mine. Everything I do is motivated by doing it right, doing it better, doing it different, answering the questions that other people couldn't."[5]

One thing was absolutely certain—another grand media experiment had failed. Examining the body count amid the carnage all around him, Zell had plenty of company in the media doghouse. Tribune's gargantuan debt load may have been the granddaddy of all IOUs in the industry, but others were struggling to make ends meet. Advertising revenue was drying up across print, broadcast, and even digital media.

A leading media bellwether, the venerable New York Times Co., saw its net income plummet in the third and fourth quarters of 2008 by 51 percent and 48 percent, respectively. The day after Tribune's bankruptcy filing, Times admitted it was negotiating with lenders to ease its own credit terms. Days later it announced a pay freeze for all nonunion employees for 2009.

Though it appeared to have enough credit to limp through 2009, Times stole an entire chapter from Zell's Tribune playbook in its fight for survival. First it hired real estate firm Cushman & Wakefield to sell the twenty-one floors it occupies in a new Renzo Piano–designed fifty-two-story corporate headquarters in Midtown Manhattan. That deal netted $225 million through what is termed a sale-leaseback arrangement. It also explored asset sales, including the *Boston Globe*. Times also sought to unload its 17.5 percent stake in the Boston Red Sox baseball franchise, the Fenway Park stadium, and a regional sports cable channel. It purchased the interest for $75 million in 2002.

At the same time, the allure of owning prime media properties showed little sign of abating as another megabillionaire was scouting Times. Mexican investor Carlos Slim, worth an estimated $67 billion—roughly equivalent to 7 percent of the total Mexican economy—pitched in to help Times, first with a $120 million loan in September 2008 and then a follow-on $250 million lifeline in early 2009.

The blood in the streets was rising faster than the price of ink, and Tribune seemed to have opened a floodgate. Gannett Co., which ran eighty-four newspapers in 2008, cut 10 percent of its workforce, or three thousand jobs, just before Christmas, after its third-quarter earnings plunged 32 percent. The McClatchy Co., the nation's second-largest newspaper publisher, with thirty titles under its wing after its $4.5 billion purchase of Knight Ridder in 2006, put the *Miami Herald*, South Florida's largest newspaper, up for sale in December 2008. *Newsday*, post–Tribune ownership, cut 5 percent, or one hundred, of its jobs in late 2008.

So what investors in their right mind would buy any media property as long as the values kept plummeting? Case in point: Cablevision, which purchased *Newsday* from Zell for $650 million in July 2008, announced it would write down the value of the paper by $375 million to $450 million, or nearly 70 percent of the purchase price, only six months later.

In one of the most radical moves, the company that runs the *Detroit Free Press* and the *Detroit News* cut home delivery of the papers to Thursdays, Fridays, and Sundays. The *Free Press* was the nation's twentieth largest paper, with a weekday circulation of nearly three hundred thousand in September 2008, and was particularly hard-hit by the challenges facing its hometown big three automakers. But the move is likely to be repeated over the coming years as the high cost of print and distribution catches up to America's dailies. For example, at one hundred years old, the *Christian Science Monitor* became the largest national daily newspaper to move to an online-only format in April 2009.

Asked if he regretted making the Tribune deal, Zell noted, "You know, my head only functions looking forward. I'm not really very good at looking behind, so consequently I don't tend to reminisce or mutilate myself as a result of past decisions. I think I made the right decision when I made it. I thought it was an appropriate investment at the time. Obviously circumstances have proven the opposite. But this too shall pass."[6]

Zell has been in business long enough to know that perception, if left unchecked, can become reality. In a have-it-now world, you're often only as good as your last deal. Even in the face of setbacks, however, Zell has a solid track record of bouncing back from mistakes. He is already mired in an international expansion campaign that is taking his entrepreneurial firebrand across the globe. And he remains relevant by being true to his contrarian nature and his instincts. Even Chapter 11s don't take those away.

15

PROFESSIONAL OPPORTUNIST

AFTER TRIBUNE, WHERE is Sam Zell headed now? Throughout his career, Zell has been down but never completely out of the game. Despite his failure with Tribune, he continues to rely on a unique ability to spot big-picture trends lingering just around the corner, and to shift the direction of his business to intercept them, often on a moment's notice. Many have bet against his intuition and perseverance, and lost.

Zell remains confident in his ability to ferret out the next untapped opportunity to add to his already enormous mountain of money. In fact, he is more active than ever, pursuing two parallel paths—one that is familiar and time tested and one that could make him a major player on the global stage.

Despite his many attempts to shed layers of his real estate legacy, Zell and the property industry are forever joined at the hip. This is the world he knows best, where he spent entire decades building up a tangible empire, then selling off chunks of it when values reached their peak. What separates Zell from the real estate broker stereotype is his ability to analyze risk better than most and to take a more holistic view of business transactions. His judgment is not clouded by an "edifice complex," which explains why he is so often inclined to distance himself from the industry's foibles.

Unfortunately, many great deal makers have an unexplained inability to see the forest for the trees, a missing trait that Zell calls "the ability to conceptualize." That helps explain the continued wild swings in the real estate industry and the inability of brokers and developers to understand what is happening in the broader markets. Zell, however, appears to have been blessed with a certain ability to grasp the concepts that others miss.

To Stephen Siegel, chairman of global brokerage at CB Richard Ellis, the world's largest real estate services firm, Zell and the real estate world have become inextricably intertwined. "He's good for the business and he puts a face on it. I think he's a very bright guy and very interesting and eccentric in some ways. His thought process is his own. He dances to his drummer and only his drummer."[1]

As globalization became a more accepted business practice in the 1990s and early 2000s, it was only a matter of time before Zell saw new opportunities that transcended the borders of the United States. Real estate, be it commercial or residential, is commonly known as a local business in which specialists devote their entire careers to learning the intricacies and machinations of specific, often small, geographic areas. But Zell has made a career out of seeing trends and pioneering new ways of thinking, always searching for that next hurdle to jump.

GOING GLOBAL

Once asked if there was one investment he would make if money were no object, Zell quickly replied, "I'd buy Brazil."

Zell was early to embrace the concept of globalization before "going global" became one of Corporate America's übertrends. Peter Linneman from Wharton helped him launch his worldwide initiatives in 1999 through a new division dubbed—surprise—Equity International. "Sam was trying to figure out if he could do non-U.S. investing, and I was a sounding board to help him go from musings to a vehicle," said Linneman. "There are opportunities out there, some very real estate–oriented and some capital market–oriented. Every country is different, every market is different. It reinforced my view that globalization in general is a powerful force for good in the world."[2]

Ultimately the Zell model for international investing was an extension of what worked in the States. Along with CEO and president Gary Garrabrant, Zell and Linneman structured Equity International (EI) as a private equity firm that would identify companies with growth potential in far-flung markets. The investment criteria were specific, disciplined, and decidedly risk-averse. EI would create investment funds—a total of four through 2008—that targeted companies in growing countries with both scale and functioning capital markets, but with limited competition. Zell schooled Garrabrant in the art of demographics, and EI focused on markets with growing middle-class consumer bases. It would also play a hands-on role in shepherding each company's management decisions.

To mitigate risk and yet move with deliberate speed, Zell and his team understood that on many occasions partnering with local talent was the only way to fly. "One of the things that we understood is that we couldn't do it on our own as we did in the United States," said Garrabrant. "That then implies that we need outstanding local operating partners. Having invested in eighteen companies around the world, in each case we have a world-class partner."[3]

Over nearly a decade, Equity International had invested in Latin America, Europe, Asia-Pacific, and the Middle East. It took three of its eighteen companies public—Homex, a leading home builder in Mexico, in June 2004; Gafisa, the second-largest home builder in Brazil, in March 2007; and BR Malls, one of the largest shopping center owners and operators in Brazil, in April 2007.

RETURN ON EQUITY

When it comes to Zell's recent crop of real estate funds, investors have been richly rewarded, reaping profits from his vision. In 2008, Zell liquidated the first of Equity International's investment funds. After nine years, the fund produced a 24.4 percent total return and generated $991 million in total gross proceeds, or more than three times the invested capital. The fund invested in real estate businesses, mainly in Mexico, and sold its last investment, Mexico Retail Properties, a shopping center developer and operator.

By 2008, Equity International's four investment funds had raised more than $1 billion in equity capital. "Our objective has been to generate superior investment returns by applying our competitive strengths as an investor, operator and professional opportunist," said Garrabrant.[4] Equity International's fourth and largest fund closed in February 2008 with nearly $500 million in equity capital commitments. Zell's ability to make money attracted some of America's top investors, including university endowments, pension plans, insurance companies, family foundations, and private investors.

MEXICO, *POR FAVOR*

One of the biggest home runs for Zell's globally focused team is Homex, the Mexican home-building operator. Here he managed to achieve a tidy return, turning his initial $100 million investment into a parlay worth around $3 billion in 2008. Again, Zell did his homework in reading the Mexican tea leaves, focusing on the increasingly strong fundamentals—scale, strong macroeconomics, expanding consumerism, housing demand, and mortgage availability.

One of the keys to making Homex work was actually an institution that Zell normally detests with a passion, the government. To help low-income Mexicans realize their dreams of home ownership, in 1972 Mexican president Luis Echeverria Álvarez established INFONAVIT, the Mexican Workers Housing Fund Institute, an autonomous organization designed to provide mortgages. By 2008, INFONAVIT had helped 4 million families buy their own homes and provided 53 percent of all mortgage loans in Mexico.

But wait, there's more. INFONAVIT also serves as the manager of Mexico's National Pension System, where workers' funds are held in separate individual accounts with minimum guaranteed annual returns. INFONAVIT is the largest manager of retirement savings in Mexico. By the end of 2007, it held nearly $43 billion in total assets, or 31 percent of all Mexican assets.

Given the projected explosion in Mexico's population and the burgeoning growth of its middle class, Zell knew his stake in Homex could put him at the vanguard of good tidings to come. It also made him somewhat of a novelty, an American deeply invested south of the border.

HIGH ON LATIN AMERICA

An expectant crowd of three hundred top real estate executives, all with vested interests in the Latin America real estate industry, were eager to hear Sam Zell espouse all things Latin America. It was October 2008, and attendees of the biannual Latin America

Conference sponsored by the Urban Land Institute were especially keen to know Zell's take on the developing economic crisis.

Just before lunch, Zell made his usual last-minute, low-key entry—head down, striding quickly through the room full of luncheon tables in his trademark blazer, dungarees, and loafers. Sitting nearby, one developer remarked, "I can't wait to hear this." Zell did not disappoint, demonstrating a surprising acumen for the ins and outs of Latin America's real estate and economic condition, combined with his trademark caustic sense of humor.

"I think I need to start with a question. What happened?" asked Zell. "Six or twelve months ago, this would have been a room full of people with cheesy grins and high-fiving." He did not bother to thinly disguise the realities of the economic recession, though Latin America was doing better than many of the more so-called developed countries.

Zell is a master at interjecting just the right analogy, always in the form of a joke, to curry audiences' favor and to reiterate the importance of learning from history. Call it a form of "leading by example." Zell likes to use the device early in his speeches, as he did on this occasion:

> It reminds me of a story I wanted to share with you, and unfortunately it's a very sad story. It's a story about a bus accident. This bus was driving through the mountains, and it went off a cliff, ended up in a ravine, and everybody died. The police came. They went to the scene of the accident. They looked at the roads, and there were no skid marks. They looked at the weather, and it was bright and sunny. And they just couldn't figure out what happened. So they went down in the ravine, and here is this bus steaming and a total wreck and all of these dead bodies were lying around. And they still couldn't figure out what happened.

Then they noticed that among the wreckage was a monkey and it was alive. They looked at each other and said, "We don't have anything else to do, why don't we ask the monkey?"

POLICE: Were you on the bus?
[Zell nods yes]
POLICE: Do you know what happened on the bus?
[Zell nods yes]
POLICE: What happened?
[Zell mimics drinking from a bottle]
POLICE: They were drinking?
[Zell nods yes]
POLICE: What else was going on?
[Zell mimics smoking marijuana]
POLICE: They were smoking dope on the bus?
[Zell nods yes]
POLICE: What else was going on?
[Zell gyrates his hips]
POLICE: They were fornicating on the bus?
[Zell nods yes]
The policemen looked at each other.
POLICE: What were you doing while all of this was going on?
[Zell mimics driving the bus]

At this the crowd broke into a spontaneous, nervous laugh. This was the icebreaker, as many in the room sensed the story was all too familiar, given their own recent brushes with the foibles of easy money. Zell echoed what many investors already knew—that the exuberance of capital invested on a worldwide scale, especially in emerging markets, including Latin America, had gotten way out of hand.

"I tell you that story because that's really what happened to all of us," Zell continued. "We were all sitting in the back of the bus. We were all having a great time. Why were we surprised? Money was flowing. IPOs were flowing. If you'd go into a *favela* [shantytown], they would know what an IPO was. You had Brazilian home builders going public. If you were a carpenter with a hammer, you were a home builder. The similarities to the dot-com era in the United States were truly incredible. There were no limits. When the price of soybeans doubled, everybody expected the price of soybeans to double again. When the price of oil went up fifty percent, it was going to go up another fifty percent."

Zell pointed to his own barometer to gauge the health of any foreign economy. His so-called McDonald's test is an unscientific way of evaluating any country's currency on a moment's notice. "The test is how much does a Big Mac, fries, and a large Coke cost in various countries around the world? Well, believe it or not, at one point, it was more expensive to buy at a McDonald's in Brazil than it was in the United States on a relative basis."

Zell then demonstrated his grasp of cultural issues, noting the effect of the U.S. economic recession, which he believed was precipitated by the fall of Wall Street investment bank Lehman Brothers in September 2008, on its southern neighbors. "We're seeing a lot of changes in Latin America that I think are going to be impacted by that. Look at the repatriation numbers to Mexico and Central America from the United States. Those repatriation numbers have gone down significantly and keep going down, which suggests that a significant percent of the illegal immigrants who have been a significant benefit to the U.S. economy have gone home. This will change the employment scenario at home and frankly will create labor shortages in certain areas in the United States."

The audience was finally getting the true measure of Zell. They suddenly realized that he was much more than just another typical "real estate investor." How many real estate moguls can easily recite immigration patterns or know the political histories of various countries, for example? Or even care?

"These are what I would call the issues that are out there that are relevant to how we got to where we are today," said Zell. "But I think it's extraordinarily important to not confuse Latin America today with Latin America ten years ago. Today Latin America has three investment-grade countries that were problem children in the past—Mexico, Chile, and Brazil.

"I don't think there is anything that is more intoxicating to a government than obtaining an investment grade. And consequently they will do whatever it takes to defend that investment grade. As Brazil raised interest rates and Mexico raised interest rates, we've seen a level of transparency that never existed in Latin America before. We see countries that in the past had allowed inflation to go wild. And we see them instead exercising significant financial discipline."

Zell's ability to stay razor focused on the factors that compose opposite ends of the economic equation—supply and demand—are what sets him apart from typical billionaires.

"As to the future, when it's all said and done, there is no greater issue than the issue of demand. As an investor, I am taking my capital on an ongoing basis and seeking places to invest it. In order for me to generate an adequate return on my capital, there has to be demand in society to support it. The developed world has little in the way of new demand. Consequently, one of the problems today is the developed world in effect replicated demand and adjusted to the lack of demand by overleveraging everything in order to gain a return," said Zell.

And this was the crux of Zell's go-global strategy—find opportunities outside the bounds of the United States that carry the proper risk/reward ratio. "In places where you have growth, you don't need to overleverage in order to achieve growth. The fact is that Latin America has little debt compared to the rest of the world. To give you an idea, Brazil has 180 million people and 300,000 mortgages. The United States has 300 million people and 400 million mortgages."

This point drew another round of laughter from the crowd. Rather than pandering to attendees to give them what they wanted to hear, Zell was using his command of the facts and figures to win plaudits. "The future is where growth exists, where the demographics tell us not only where demand is today but where there will be demand tomorrow."

Zell was in full "love guru" mode, and sticking to a format that is standard fare in his speeches—the opening joke, his command of the facts, and finally, the nitty-gritty takeaways the audience was waiting to hear all along.

"We're seeing fiscal discipline in Latin America. It's almost like the ultimate oxymoron, but it's happening and it's very positive," he said. "In the end there will be a focus and a flight to quality. If there was ever a time in history where 'idea' companies have no role, it certainly is today. And yet at the same time, throughout Latin America we see enormous successful and productive companies that are selling at dramatic discounts to their inherent value. I believe this is a temporary phenomenon, and I believe it will be looked back upon in the next twelve months as an extraordinary opportunity to take advantage of the growth opportunities in today's business in Latin America."

Zell emboldened the crowd, reinforcing exactly why he was the keynote speaker at a large Latin America conference of his peers. "I believe that Latin America, relatively speaking, will outperform the developed world. I believe there's a great future. I believe that Latin America, as opposed to being profligate, has been very careful. Last week we dramatically increased our position in Gafisa, and we expect to increase our position in other investments in Latin America, particularly Brazil and Mexico, going forward."

And finally, he delivered the bold crescendo, a flurry of a finish, Zell style. "This is the time that tries all men's souls. This is the time when we find out if we really have balls. But this is also the time where extraordinary fortunes will be made, extraordinary opportunities will be taken advantage of. When it's all said and done, recognizing true value and having the staying power to be there at the end is what it's all about."

Zell's speech was followed by a brief question-and-answer period that provided further insight into his investment mind. Asked how the Tribune investment was going, his tongue-in-cheek reply told much about his state of mind on that sore subject. "Well, this is a Latin America conference so I will confine my remarks to that topic. I can tell you, though, that the only thing worse than being in Latin American stocks right now is to own a newspaper."

Another question, about the state of investing in Argentina, drew one of Zell's zingers, which he dispenses in ample amounts. "I need to keep my hands in my pockets while I'm talking to make sure my money isn't stolen [laughter]. The Argentines have done worse than the times of the Perons, and the Perons were pretty awful. This latest confiscation of the pension funds . . . I mean, they are destroying any confidence the people had in their government, if they had any before. Argentines seem to think they can be unconnected to the rest of the world, and they're finding out real quickly how connected they really are. They've done everything to discourage capital there."

Typically, Zell fields at least one question that is at the heart of why so many people yearn to hear him speak. They want to know "The One Thing" that will make them more successful, even if they only garner a fraction of Zell's wealth in their lifetime. Unfortunately for them, Zell the articulator is never fully able to satisfy their curiosity. Which of course keeps them coming back for more.

"I don't have any magic formulas," he says. "I'm extraordinarily focused. I read five newspapers a day and six magazines a week, and I'm constantly collecting information from both what I read and the people I talk to, and somehow or other that all gives me a perspective."

Ask his opinion on what international markets are most attractive, for example, and you get an in-depth, informed analysis. "When I look at the whole continent, I keep coming back to Mexico and Brazil being the two arenas where scale is achievable, and if your goals are to create world-class entities, then you can only do that with scale. I think China has possibilities. I'd probably limit myself to those three at the moment," said Zell. "As far as Russia is concerned, I think they've been taking lessons from Argentina. Or maybe Argentina has been taking lessons from Russia. But kleptomania is obviously involved in both.

"We have found a lot of terrific smaller companies that we could invest in, and we could give them capital to grow. I've been telling everyone for the past ten years that when investing in emerging markets, you make a deal with the devil. You are basically trading growth for the rule of law. We take great pride in the fact that in the last ten years we've never seen the inside of a Latin American courtroom and don't intend to, moving forward. You succeed or you fail based on who your partners are."

Zell was finally asked to address one of the largest elephants in the room, the U.S. presidential election and the impact of U.S. politics on cross-border relations. Quick on his feet, he deftly swung the crowd in his favor.

"I'm not really a big supporter of walls," noted Zell. "One, they don't work, and two, the United States is and always has been the melting pot for people from all over the world. I was born ninety days after my parents came to this country. So I understand maybe better than a lot of you in the room what it means to grow up as an immigrant in the United States.

"But what I would also tell you is that my standing here today is a validation of what America really stands for. It stands for opportunity. It stands for challenge. It stands for a level playing field. I believe all of our policies about immigration make no sense and we should be focused on 'How do we make these people citizens?' because the ones coming to this country are exactly the kind of people that have always been attracted to this country and therefore made this country the most prosperous in the world."[5]

CHINA-BOUND

Zell would never be accused of being a "bleeding edge" investor, meaning he would take a flyer on a potentially high return if it meant extraordinary risk and years of losses before achieving a profit. But he has been known to arrive well ahead of the other guests at many an investment party.

Take his entry into China. His first investment there was in September 2006, when he bought a 14 percent interest for $10 million in Xinyuan Real Estate, a Chinese home builder based in Zhengzhou, the capital city of Henan Province. In December 2007, Xinyuan held its initial public offering on the New York Stock Exchange (NYSE:XIN), the first U.S. listing by a Chinese home builder. Zell and his team used the knowledge they had gained from their Latin American experience.

"No one's ever heard of it, no one can even spell it," said Equity International CEO Garrabrant, referring to the Xinyuan firm. But it is hard not to see the potential in China, the world's fastest growing economy, especially as the country's secondary or "tier II" cities outside Shanghai and Beijing are set to experience rapid growth, thanks to a burgeoning middle class, demand for home ownership, and availability of mortgage financing.

"My first trip [to Zhengzhou] I discovered a big tent in the middle of the city with seven or eight hundred people clutching little numbers, and as the numbers were called, extended families would rush the stage to get in line to wait for their opportunity to get fifteen minutes to pick out their home. These are high-rise homes, and we sold out one of our projects there that day. It just speaks to the Econ 101 aspect to this emerging-markets home building, which is that the demand is far in excess of the supply," said Garrabrant.[6]

Equity International upped its Chinese presence in September 2007, investing in Shanghai Jingrui Properties Co., Ltd., a privately held home-building company headquartered in Shanghai. Jingrui focuses on building and selling homes to middle-income and upper-middle-income buyers in Shanghai and the Yangtze River Delta, but is pursuing developments in tier II and tier III cities across China. It has operations in five cities, including Shanghai, Chongqing, Xi'an, Changzhou, and Zhoushan.

In 2008, Zell ventured into China's warehouse sector through an investment in Shanghai Yupei Group Co., Ltd., a privately held warehousing and logistics real estate company headquartered in Shanghai. Though considered small by U.S. industrial real estate standards, with five buildings totaling over 1 million square feet of space in four cities, Yupei is emerging as a leading domestic landlord within the logistics and warehousing real estate sector, focused on leasing space to high-quality tenants and third-party logistics service providers.

MIDDLE EAST PIECE

Zell obviously could not overlook the oil-rich Middle East as an investment target. Surprisingly at ease among sheiks and overlords alike, his strategy here, too, was unconventional. Rather than focus on high-profile companies and projects, he carefully studied the trends shaping the region. He settled on Egypt.

His first Middle East partnership came in September 2006 with homebuilder Orascom Housing Communities, a unit of Cairo-based Orascom Development Holding, a huge company that builds entire towns in Egypt and is developing in Morocco, Oman, the United Arab Emirates, Switzerland, Jordan, and Mauritius. "We wouldn't be in Egypt, were it not for them," said Garrabrant. "Egypt is similar to Mexico twenty years ago."[7]

By early 2009, Garrabrant was thanking his lucky stars that no matter what markets Equity International entered, it did not have to rely on borrowing money to invest, thanks to Zell's insistence on sticking to a conservative business plan a decade earlier. "Our independence of debt serves us well today. We run an unleveraged business," said Garrabrant.[8]

Jetting around the globe with Zell opened Garrabrant's eyes to future opportunities, particularly in India, North Africa, and Vietnam. Investing in emerging markets is still fraught with unseen perils, however, as evidenced by the surprising terrorist attacks on two prominent hotels in Mumbai, India, in November 2008.

MILKING IT?

One of Zell's more offbeat international investments saw him venture farther afield than ever, both geographically and conceptually. It also speaks to the power and significance that business relationships have in Zell's world. In October 2008, he took a smallish $5 million stake in a company called A2 Corporation, based in New Zealand, on the other side of the world from Chicago. For that sum, minuscule by Zell standards, he snapped up 50 million shares of A2's stock, or 13.8 percent of the company.

Fans of international economies know that New Zealand is the world's largest exporter of dairy products (some 33 percent in 2007) and is the fifth largest cheese exporter. As a player in that industry, A2 Corp.'s claim to fame was a patented DNA test, whereby a hair plucked from a cow's tail—no joke—could identify whether it carries special A2 beta-casein proteins. These cows are used to produce what is known as A2 milk, which is branded as a healthy alternative to standard milk, known as A1. A2 Corp. claimed that scientific tests proved that traditional A1 milk could contribute to childhood ailments, including type 1 diabetes, heart disease, and autism.

Zell actually stumbled upon the A2 investment, as he so often does, through connections with his investment partners. As part of his shifting global investing acumen, in November 2007 he invested in two retirement-housing companies, Renaissance Lifecare and Sanctuary Residences, which developed, purchased, and operated high-end retirement housing in the United Kingdom, Australia, and New Zealand. The founder of those companies, Cliff Cook, also happened to hold a major interest in A2 Corp. as its chairman. Zell was easily convinced that a small stake in the company could pay off long-term. Though A2 Corp. was still losing money at the end of 2008, it had paid off its long-term debt, and distribution of A2 milk was growing in Australia and South Korea.

Quirky, offbeat investments like A2 Corp. add spice to Zell's ever-expanding global empire but will not be the primary drivers of his business growth in the years to come. Without a doubt, 2008 was a tough year in his professional life, filled with milestones he would love to forget but which will cling to him for months and possibly years to come, especially as Tribune slogs its way through bankruptcy. He understands that reputations, which can take decades to build and nurture, can be easily and indiscriminately washed away in a matter of moments.

Still, Zell will not compromise or alter his brash, against-the-grain investment style. He remains a walking contradiction, a private individual who yearns to preach his message of entrepreneurism and independent thinking. Think of him as the business community's version of *American Idol*'s opinionated character Simon Cowell—saying what he thinks, driven by a passion for his work, and caring little about how the rest of the world may view him here and now. Loathed and loved, depending on your perspective.

Fast approaching an age when most business professionals start to seriously consider retirement—Zell turned sixty-eight in September 2009—he is more active than ever and yet more cognizant of his mortality. "I am old enough to be concerned about my legacy, concerned about who I am and what people will think of me in the future," said Zell. Asked what message he would like to have on his tombstone, Zell responded without thinking: "'He was a man of his word.' Most important of all, whether it be in the business world, the philanthropic world, or the sports world, I want to make a difference. That's what motivates me."[9]

EPILOGUE

CERTAINLY THE ECONOMIC crisis that began in earnest in late 2008 had a variety of impacts on Zell's businesses. The credit crunch stalled his sale of the Chicago Cubs for a time, but he still managed to tiptoe through the broken bodies on Wall Street to close a record-setting deal. Pressure mounted on the entire publishing industry's advertising revenues, including Tribune's, but at least its status as the "lead dog" in the race to bankruptcy offered some measure of protection from the wolves at the door.

At the same time, the subprime residential mortgage mess seriously stalled the American appetite for home ownership, which fostered a burgeoning renter's market that would benefit Zell's Equity Residential apartment firm. His Equity Lifestyle Properties also saw gains as more Americans took to the road in their RVs and found mobile-home communities more affordable. Having a diversified portfolio of investments helps mitigate the inevitable peaks and valleys of business cycles, and Zell never keeps many of his eggs in any one basket for too long.

There were still periodic glimmers of hope for the flagging newspaper business. Apparently what newspapers need more than anything else is a presidential election every year. Though Zell was anything but a staunch Obama supporter—his political leanings tend to be more conservative Republican than Democrat— certainly his Tribune enterprise was rewarded by Obama's big U.S. presidential win. The *Chicago Tribune* ginned up the presses to distribute hundreds of thousands of extra copies of the inauguration edition, while the *Los Angeles Times* sold a hundred thousand more copies than it did on a normal Wednesday. Single copies of papers were selling for as much as $50 each on the auction site eBay.

The Tribune bankruptcy did little to stem the tongue-in-cheek style of Tribune's parade of press releases, and Zell is not likely to abandon his trademark addiction to self-deprecation and humor. Nor is he likely to stray far from his grave-dancing real estate roots. Considering the magnitude of the worldwide economic downturn and the levels of distress in the real estate markets, Zell is easily capable of launching large-scale opportunity funds, along the lines of the Zell/Merrill Lynch funds of the 1980s, to take advantage of market conditions. After all, banking relationships are most easily mended when the promise of profits is at hand.

Deep into the financial crisis in mid-2009, Zell was buying up distressed loans from banks and troubled companies alike. It looked a lot like the 1970s and '80s all over again. And the grave dancer, with money in hand, was once again buying while others were scrambling.

Despite the Tribune bankruptcy, Zell will also maintain his status as an arbiter of sage investment advice. Bloomberg, CNBC, and countless other media outlets trot out the "exclusives" anytime Zell deigns an interview. Apparently the Tribune experience added to his mystique and fostered his popularity as a generator of "good copy."

One favorite topic is what led to the global downturn in the first place, the housing crisis. "I wasn't shocked by the extent of [the residential real estate collapse] because there was absolute unequivocal blind faith in the value of a house and the belief that it would just keep going up forever," he noted in late 2008. "Part of what we've all lived through in the last year and a half is breaking the holy grail of housing. The truth of the matter is we've had numerous housing slides in the past. The only difference is, except for the Depression, you've never had a country-wide reduction in housing at the same time."[1]

While many commentators hemmed and hawed about where to place the blame for the housing crisis, Zell laid the responsibility for the mess squarely on the back of the American ideal of home ownership. "Look at history. I've been in the real estate business for almost fifty years. During that period of time, the government has three or four times attempted to move the percentage of owned housing above sixty-two percent. And every time we have a government program or a government encourage an increase in housing ownership beyond sixty-two percent, we have a disaster. The latest one took it to sixty-nine percent. The other ones only took it to sixty-six percent. And each time, total disaster. It's a wonderful goal; everyone should own their own house. But the reality is we keep seeing over and over again that only sixty-three percent of the people who want a home ever can afford it."[2]

Ever the optimist, Zell reasons that positive mental attitude, coupled with a healthy dose of pragmatism, will always win the day. "The biggest issue overall is to focus on confidence, because if people have no confidence, they will not make commitments. And if they make no commitments, for sure our economy will suffer.

Despite the stock market going down, a lot of people fornicated last night and are producing children. And a whole bunch came across the border. The net result is household formations are growing at over a million a year right now.[3]

"See, I didn't say 'fuck,' I said 'fornicate.' Don't I get points for that?"

APPENDIX

CHAPTER 8

Full text of filing by the Chandler Trusts to the Securities & Exchange Commission by attorney William Stinehart Jr.:

CHANDLER TRUST NO. 1

CHANDLER TRUST NO. 2

June 13, 2006

The Board of Directors
The Tribune Company
435 North Michigan Avenue
Chicago, Illinois 60611

Dear Directors:

The Chandler Trusts do not intend to tender any shares in response to the tender offer announced by Tribune on May 30, 2006. The Trusts believe that the process by which the offer was presented and considered by the Tribune Board was fundamentally flawed, and that the offer is a purely financial device that fails altogether to address the real business issues facing Tribune. Prompt and meaningful strategic action is required to preserve the premium value of the company's franchises.

As you know, the basic strategic premise of the Tribune/ Times Mirror merger was that the cross-ownership of multiple premium major media properties in the nation's three largest media outlets would provide a platform to produce above-industry performance for both its newspaper and broadcast assets and for strong growth in inter- active and other media opportunities. This strategy has failed and the regulatory change anticipated at the time of the merger to make legal the permanent cross-ownership of certain key assets has not occurred. Over the past two years, Tribune has significantly underperformed industry averages and there is scant evidence to suggest the next two years will be any different. Clearly, it is time for prompt, comprehensive action.

We believe management and its advisors created a false sense of urgency in representing to directors that immediate action was required on the self-tender transaction. As a result, the Board's action was hasty and ill-informed. Tactical alternatives were superficially listed and dismissed without addressing the failure of the company's fundamental strategy or its poor performance. Prudence should have required that management first determine a cogent and realistic strategy for restoring the value of Tribune's businesses and assets prior to creating a financial structure that limits strategic options.

Furthermore, it is now apparent that the credibility of
the company's management and the company's standing
in the credit markets has been harmed by the proposed
recapitalization and the uncertainty it highlighted as to
strategic direction. Without prompt action, all of this could
prove very costly to the company and its stockholders in
the future.

In addition to the failure of its primary strategy, the
company is confronted with a fundamental erosion in
both of its core businesses and the consequences of failing
to invest aggressively in growing new businesses. In the
face of these serious challenges, management has failed
to generate a viable strategic response, allowing value to
deteriorate and creating a need for decisive action.

- *First*, Tribune must find a way to separate the
newspaper business from television broadcasting. By far
the most expeditious and effective way to accomplish this
is through a tax-free spin-off, which management and
the Board have been considering—without action—for
many months. Among other things, management should
diligently explore the possibility of arranging for a major
private equity firm to make a significant investment in the
television company and act as its *"sponsor."*
- *Second*, Tribune should begin promptly exploring
other strategic alternatives, including breaking up and
selling, or disposing in tax-free spin-offs, some or all of its
newspaper properties, or alternatively, the possibility of an
acquisition of Tribune as a whole at an attractive premium.
- *Third*, we call upon the Board to appoint a committee
of independent directors as soon as possible to oversee
a thorough review and evaluation of the management,

business and strategic issues facing Tribune and to promptly execute alternatives to restore and enhance stockholder value.

Given the risk of continued deterioration in the company's primary businesses, if a separation of the newspaper and broadcast businesses or other strategic steps relative to the newspaper business cannot be accomplished by the end of the year, then the possibility of an acquisition of Tribune as a whole should take priority.

Tribune's Strategic Failure Has Had Disastrous Effects.

Tribune's strategic missteps are now reflected in a market valuation multiple that is well below its peers. Management's proposed response—the self-tender—is simply a financial device that increases the company's risk profile and undercuts the financial flexibility necessary to address the company's fundamental challenges. We believe that this sequencing—financial structure in advance of strategy—is backwards.

Management's operational response (yet another new round of cost-cutting) is subject to serious execution risk and offers little to spur revenue growth and invigorate the newspaper franchises. As is shown in detail below, management has been and is once again acquiescing to sub-par growth in return for short-term cash flow. Morale at many of the newspapers is already quite low and will be driven lower with a new round of cost cuts.

In announcing the self-tender offer, Tribune repeated previous statements about seeking growth through Internet initiatives, a comment that has little credibility following a history of cost-cutting and retrenchment in these areas, its failure to purchase and invest in such businesses at the pace of comparable companies with more successful interactive businesses and its decision to limit local interactive growth initiatives at the newspapers in favor of a *"one size fits all"* corporate approach. Moreover, a growth strategy that relies on partially owned, externally managed ventures is operationally tenuous and value limiting as the financial markets do not recognize the upside of such investments.

The gravity of management's failure to address fundamental strategic issues is apparent from the precipitous decline in stock value over the past three and a half years. As the following chart summarizes, since the beginning of 2003 (when current management of Tribune was put in place), the value of Tribune's stock has declined over 38%—substantially worse than both the newspaper peer group (down 8.8%) and the broadcasting peer group (down 29.0%).

These results have been disastrous to investors. Over the past two years, the value of Tribune's stock has declined by nearly half. While both the newspaper and broadcasting sectors have been under pressure, Tribune management has had little response.

One of the core strategies underlying the merger with Times-Mirror was the synergistic growth opportunities of cross-ownership. Unfortunately, this strategy has failed to produce results. For example, *"In 2001, then-CEO John Madigan told BusinessWeek he expected Tribune Media Net—a unit created to sell cross-platform and cross-property ad packages—to lure an incremental $200 million in national advertising in 2005. In 2004 the company netted an incremental $85 million from such sales—and has since*

*stopped quantifying Tribune Media Net's performance, says
a spokesman."* (BusinessWeek, June 11, 2006). Not only
did synergistic growth from cross-ownership not appear,
but investments in growth suffered. Other publishers, such
as E.W. Scripps and New York Times, have aggressively
pursued investments in growing [I]nternet properties that
hold promise for substantial future growth, while Tribune
has primarily managed a declining asset base for short-
term cash flow.

Since 2003, Tribune's revenue and EBITDA have
underperformed its peers and, unfortunately, analyst
estimates for the next two years indicate that they expect
the same bleak picture. These below-average results
have prevailed in both the newspaper publishing and
broadcasting divisions, as evidenced by the . . . tables[.]

Not only has Tribune underperformed the industry
averages, but the company has lagged business segment
performance for *each* of the companies in the comparable
list over the last two years. Notwithstanding the forecasted
cross-ownership benefits, Tribune still underperformed
comparable companies, even those with a similar asset
mix favoring larger markets. This trend is only expected to
continue for the next two years as shown in the . . .
charts[.]

As a result of this continued underperformance, Tribune
not only trades at a steep discount to its peers but to its
intrinsic value, as measured by a sum-of-the-parts analysis.
Morgan Stanley and Bear Stearns research suggest a
breakup value of $42 per share, or a 50% premium over
the pre-tender price of $28 per share. Prudential analysts
suggest a similar price, pegging the value at $43 per
share. Reflecting the premium value of the company's

properties, analysts at Ariel Capital, one of Tribune's biggest stockholders, figure that Tribune shares would be worth $44 to $46 per share in a breakup involving a subsequent sale of the parts (Wall Street Journal, June 9, 2006). These four data points define a range of values resulting from sum-of-the-parts of $42 to $46 per share.

Management Projections of a Turnaround are Unfounded.

Much as they have in the previous two years, management doggedly projects a turnaround, with steady revenue and operating cash flow growth over the next four years. This projected turnaround is hard to believe with no proposed change in strategy and little prospect for an upturn in the core businesses. Management has already revised estimates down since December 2005, suggesting the likely direction of future changes. With the current plan in place, we believe the risk of further deterioration in print and broadcast outweighs the projected growth in interactive, a segment that, while growing, still makes up less than 9% of revenues (including joint ventures). Since analysts do not share management's outlook, we believe Tribune should disclose both the projections and the related downside analysis presented to the board, so that investors can evaluate them independently and make their own informed decision.

In addition, the announced tender fails to increase the intrinsic value of Tribune's assets while introducing risks that were barely acknowledged in the Board's perfunctory consideration of the leveraged recapitalization. Even if the optimistic assumptions of management's latest profit forecast were realized in full, management's projection of

Tribune's year 2010 stock price translates into only $33 to $35 per share in today's value, assuming an appropriate equity return, expected dividends and no decline in valuation multiples. As an upside return from a very risky plan, this is far from satisfactory.

By contrast, Lauren Fine of Merrill Lynch expects Tribune EBITDA to decline at 1.3% per year over the next 5 years. That outcome in today's dollars would be $26 per share at constant multiples and $21 per share with a contraction of one turn in Tribune's EBITDA multiple (a likely scenario with that level of performance). Even this is far from the most draconian view of Tribune's future. An economic slowdown comparable to that in 2001 and 2002, combined with management's continued failure to deal with secular challenges, will leave Tribune in serious risk of violating its loan covenants.

This relationship of risk and reward inherent in the management plans and strategy is uninspiring to shareholders at best; and the company's lack of a strategy to derive maximum value from its assets is unacceptable. This is a situation that demands prompt action by the Board of Directors.

Decisive Action is Required.

It is now apparent that Tribune must find a way, at a minimum, to separate the newspaper business from television broadcasting. By far the most expeditious and effective way to accomplish this is through a tax-free spin-off, which management and the Board have been considering—without action—for many months. As an independent company, the television broadcast business will have opportunities for a merger or acquisition that could bring substantial value to shareholders.

We believe management should broaden its thinking and process. Among other things, management should diligently explore the possibility of arranging for a major private equity firm to make a significant investment in the television company and act as its *"sponsor."* By so doing, the financial resources available to the television business can be substantially enhanced with leadership from the sponsor firm providing much-needed strength to management.

The primary expressed objection to a third quarter spin-off of the broadcasting business appears to be the desire to wait to see how the new CW network performs. This is not a valid basis for inaction. If the network performs well, those shareholders who retain the spun-off shares of the broadcast company will fully realize the benefit. If it performs poorly, there is no reason to think that Tribune shareholders will be advantaged by the fact that the business is embedded in the present Tribune corporate structure. On the other hand, a spin-off will provide shareholders a choice of whether or not to retain this risk exposure. Further, a sponsored spin-off creates the opportunity to augment capital of the spin-off broadcast company by taking investment from a private equity firm. This reduces risk and provides the added benefit of a committed financial partner.

We also believe that Tribune should begin promptly exploring other strategic alternatives, including breaking up and selling, or disposing in tax-free spin-offs, some or all of its newspaper properties, and the possibility of an acquisition of Tribune as a whole at an attractive premium. The primary operational benefit of spin-offs with the right combination of assets will be to incent and enhance focus of the new entities' management teams and to allow for growth strategies that are freed from the corporate *"one size fits all"* approach, with particular emphasis on capitalizing on local competitive advantages, including interactive initiatives. We believe that it is not too late for the right combination of assets to deliver significantly more long-term value than the current plan. But, given the deterioration in the current businesses as presently configured, expeditious action is called for.

In addition, in light of inquiries received from very credible private equity firms, and the very liquid, low cost financing markets, it seems quite likely that a leveraged buyout could be accomplished at a price in excess of $35 per share. This would provide shareholders cash value at or above the high end value implied in management's plans without any exposure to the huge downside risk of the as yet unaddressed fundamental strategic challenges of Tribune's business. If a separation of broadcasting and newspapers cannot be accomplished by year end, the company should actively pursue inquiries from private equity firms.

Moving Forward.

As you know, Tribune's tax counsel have advised that the present structure of the two TMCT entities is a significant obstacle to accomplishing a tax-free spin-off of the television broadcast business (or any other Tribune business). Similarly, the TMCTs are a substantial impediment to an acquisition of Tribune because of the more than 51 million shares of Tribune common stock and over $500 million of preferred stock presently trapped inside the TMCTs. Notwithstanding that 80% of those shares are accounted for as being treasury stock, for legal purposes they are outstanding and must be paid for in any Tribune acquisition. This is a state of affairs that we believe is disadvantageous to all stockholders.

We have had extensive discussions with Tribune management, seeking agreement on the terms for substantially unwinding TMCT by way of a redemption of most of Tribune's ownership interest. We did not seek any advantage for the Chandler Trusts in these discussions. In fact, to resolve a major difference regarding the value of real estate held by TMCT, we offered Tribune an option to purchase the real estate at a value $150 million dollars <u>less</u> than the amount that Tribune's appraiser determined to be its value to Tribune. The Chandler Trusts remain willing to proceed with the TMCT redemption on terms that are fair and reasonable for all shareholders of Tribune. At an appropriate time, the Trusts are willing to enter into similar discussions with respect to TMCT II.

To make the obvious point, through their direct and indirect holdings, the Trusts are the largest investor in the company, and, more than any other shareholder, it is in their interests to see that either current value is maximized or a value enhancing strategic repositioning occurs.

We all have a vital interest in a cooperative effort among Tribune's Board, major stockholders like the Chandler Trusts and all other stockholders. It is time for a strategic course of action to be set for Tribune, and stockholders apparently concur given the movement in the company's stock price last week. As one shareholder said, *"the train has definitely left the station but no one knows where it's going."* (New York Times, June 9, 2006).

As noted above, we call upon the Board to promptly appoint a committee of independent directors to oversee a thorough review of the issues facing Tribune and to take prompt decisive action to enhance stockholder value. In our view, such a committee must review all of the areas noted above, including management issues and potential strategic alternatives. It is essential, in our judgment, that the committee of independent directors retain a financial advisor and legal counsel of their choice that have no material prior or ongoing relationship with Tribune.

We are prepared to work directly and cooperatively with such a committee to further our common objective of maximizing value and halting what now appears to be an inexorable slide in value of Tribune's businesses. If timely action is not taken, however, we intend to begin actively pursuing possible changes in Tribune's management and other transactions to enhance the value realized by all Tribune stockholders by engaging with other stockholders and other parties.

Sincerely yours,

CHANDLER TRUST NO. 1 and

CHANDLER TRUST NO. 2

By:/s/ William Stinehart, Jr.

Name: William Stinehart, Jr.

Title: Trustee

CHAPTER 9

Full text of Tribune Company's press release announcing the sale of Tribune to Sam Zell:

Tribune to Go Private for $34 Per Share

Employee Stock Ownership Plan (ESOP) Created
Sam Zell to Invest, Join Board
Chicago Cubs and Comcast SportsNet Interest to be Sold

CHICAGO, April 2, 2007—With the completion of its strategic review process, Tribune Company (NYSE:TRB) today announced a transaction which will result in the company going private and Tribune shareholders receiving $34 per share. Sam Zell is supporting the transaction with a $315 million investment. Shareholders will receive their consideration in a two-stage transaction.

Upon completion of the transaction, the company will be privately held, with an Employee Stock Ownership Plan (ESOP) holding all of Tribune's then-outstanding common stock and Zell holding a subordinated note and a warrant entitling him to acquire 40 percent of Tribune's common stock. Zell will join the Tribune board upon completion of his initial investment and will become chairman when the merger closes.

The first stage of the transaction is a cash tender offer for approximately 126 million shares at $34 per share. The tender offer will be funded by incremental borrowings and a $250 million investment from Sam Zell. It is anticipated to be completed in the second quarter of 2007. The second stage is a merger expected to close in the fourth quarter of 2007 in which the remaining publicly-held shares will receive $34 per share. Zell will make an additional investment of $65 million in connection with the merger, bringing his investment in Tribune to $315 million.

The board of directors of Tribune, on the recommendation of a special committee comprised entirely of independent directors, has approved the agreements and will recommend Tribune shareholder approval. Representatives of the Chandler Trusts on the board abstained from voting as directors. However, the Chandler Trusts have agreed to vote in favor of the transaction.

The agreements reached between Tribune, the ESOP and Zell and announced today include the following transactions:

- The ESOP will immediately purchase $250 million of newly issued Tribune common stock for $28 per share.
- Zell will invest $250 million in Tribune and join its board of directors. Of this initial investment, $50 million will purchase approximately 1.5 million newly issued shares of Tribune common stock for $34 per share and $200 million will purchase a note exchangeable for common stock at a $34 per share exchange price. The Zell investment will be completed upon expiration or early termination of the Hart-Scott-Rodino waiting period, subject to other customary conditions.
- Tribune will launch a tender offer to repurchase approximately 126 million shares of its common stock for $34 per share, returning approximately $4.3 billion of capital to shareholders. The tender offer will be subject to the completion of financing arrangements, receipt of a

solvency opinion and other customary conditions; it is expected to be completed in the second quarter of 2007.

- Following the tender offer, Tribune and the ESOP will merge and all remaining Tribune stock will be converted to cash at $34 per share. The merger will be subject to Tribune shareholder approval, FCC and other regulatory approvals, receipt of financing and a solvency opinion, and other conditions reflected in the definitive agreements that will be filed later this week with the SEC. If the merger has not closed by Jan. 1, 2008, shareholders will receive an additional amount of cash based upon an 8 percent annualized "ticking fee" that will accrue from Jan. 1, 2008, until the closing.
- Up to the time of shareholder approval, Tribune's board of directors will be entitled, subject to specified conditions, to consider unsolicited alternative proposals that may lead to a superior proposal. In the event such a superior proposal is selected, the break-up fee to Zell would be $25 million.
- In conjunction with the execution of these agreements, Tribune will suspend its regular quarterly dividend.
- Upon completion of the merger, Zell's initial $250 million investment will be redeemed and Zell will make a new investment through the purchase of a subordinated note for $225 million with an 11-year maturity and a warrant for $90 million with a 15-year maturity. The warrant can be exercised by Zell at any time to acquire 40 percent of Tribune's common stock for an aggregate exercise price initially of $500 million.
- The company will be led by a board of directors with an independent majority. Dennis FitzSimons, as Tribune

president and chief executive officer, will remain a member of the board, along with at least five independent directors and an additional director affiliated with Zell.

"The strategic review process was rigorous and thorough," said William A. Osborn, Tribune's lead director and chairman of the special committee that was charged with overseeing the company's evaluation of strategic alternatives. "The committee reviewed a variety of third-party proposals and alternatives for restructuring the company. We determined that this course of action provides the greatest certainty for achieving the highest value for all shareholders and is in the best interest of investors and employees."

Osborn added, "In particular, we took into account a letter received from Messrs. Broad and Burkle, dated March 29, 2007, expressing their willingness to enter into a definitive contract offering shareholders $34 per share—that is, the same price as the ESOP/Zell plan. We considered this letter in the light of prior discussions with Messrs. Broad and Burkle and the completed negotiations of definitive agreements with Zell and the ESOP trustee."

Sam Zell said, "I am delighted to be associated with Tribune Company, which I believe is a world-class publishing and broadcasting enterprise. As a long-term investor, I look forward to partnering with the management and employees as we build on the great heritage of Tribune Company."

"The steps announced today will deliver a positive outcome for all Tribune shareholders, including our employees," said Dennis FitzSimons, Tribune chairman, president and chief executive officer. "We welcome Sam Zell to the Tribune board and know that he will bring valuable insights from his successful career."

FitzSimons added, "As a private company, Tribune will have greater flexibility to transform our publishing/interactive and broadcasting businesses with an eye toward long-term growth. Importantly, our employees will have a significant stake in the company's future. Tribune's local media businesses have succeeded through the years by serving their communities well, by providing great journalism and programming to readers, viewers and listeners and by creating value for advertisers who need to reach them. That will not change."

Tribune Employee Retirement Plans

Beginning Jan. 1, 2008, eligible Tribune employees will participate in three retirement plans:

- ESOP: The newly-created ESOP will be funded solely through company contributions. Those contributions will be invested in shares of Tribune stock (the private company), which will be allocated each year among eligible employees' accounts in the ESOP trust. The first allocation, for the year 2008, will be made in early 2009. The company initially anticipates an annual allocation of approximately 5 percent, based on employees' eligible compensation. GreatBanc Trust Company will serve as the ESOP trustee, and the ESOP will be administered by a board-appointed employee benefits committee.

- Cash Balance Plan: A cash balance plan will be funded entirely by the company and provide a 3 percent annual allocation to each eligible employee's cash balance plan account.
- Existing 401(k) Plans: Eligible employees will continue having the opportunity to contribute a portion of their pre-tax earnings to 401(k) accounts.
- There will be no change to pension benefits previously earned by employees and retirees. Tribune sponsors defined-benefit pension plans for approximately 37,000 participants. As of year-end 2006, the pension plans had assets of over $1.7 billion and were overfunded by more than $200 million.

"Going forward, employees participating in the ESOP will be invested alongside Sam Zell, one of today's most successful investors. With the additional plans, Tribune employees will have a well-rounded package of retirement benefits," said FitzSimons.

Financing Commitments

Tribune has financing commitments from Citigroup, Merrill Lynch and JPMorgan Chase to fund the transactions. In the first stage, Tribune will raise $7.0 billion of new debt of which $4.2 billion will be used to complete the tender offer and the remaining $2.8 billion will be used to refinance existing bank credit facilities. In the second stage, Tribune will raise an additional $4.2 billion of debt which will be used to buy all the remaining outstanding shares of the company. Tribune's existing publicly-traded bonds are expected to remain outstanding.

Sale of the Chicago Cubs

Separately, Tribune announced that following the 2007 baseball season, it will sell the Chicago Cubs and the company's 25 percent interest in Comcast SportsNet Chicago. The sale of the Cubs is subject to the approval of Major League Baseball, and is expected to be completed in the fourth quarter of 2007. Proceeds will be used to pay down debt.

Advisors

The financial advisors to the company and its board of directors were Merrill Lynch and Citigroup. The financial advisor to the special committee was Morgan Stanley. Legal counsel to the company and its board of directors were Wachtell Lipton Rosen & Katz, Sidley Austin LLP and, for ESOP matters, McDermott Will & Emery. Legal counsel to the special committee was Skadden Arps. Duff & Phelps served as financial advisor to the ESOP trustee and its legal counsel was K & L Gates. The financial advisor to Zell was JPMorgan Chase, and legal counsel to Zell were Jenner & Block, Arnold & Porter, Morgan Lewis, and Dow Lohnes.

CHAPTER 10

Full text of "The Journalists' Creed" by Walter Williams, founder of the University of Missouri School of Journalism:

The Journalists' Creed

I believe in the profession of journalism.

I believe that the public journal is a public trust; that all

connected with it are, to the full measure of their responsibility, trustees for the public; that acceptance of a lesser
service than the public service is betrayal of this trust.

I believe that clear thinking and clear statement, accu-
racy and fairness are fundamental to good journalism.

I believe that a journalist should write only what he
holds in his heart to be true.

I believe that suppression of the news, for any consideration other than the welfare of society, is indefensible.

I believe that no one should write as a journalist what
he would not say as a gentleman; that bribery by one's
own pocketbook is as much to be avoided as bribery by
the pocketbook of another; that individual responsibility
may not be escaped by pleading another's instructions or
another's dividends.

I believe that advertising, news and editorial columns
should alike serve the best interests of readers; that a
single standard of helpful truth and cleanness should pre-
vail for all; that the supreme test of good journalism is the
measure of its public service.

I believe that the journalism which succeeds best—
and best deserves success—fears God and honors Man;
is stoutly independent, unmoved by pride of opinion or
greed of power, constructive, tolerant but never careless,
self-controlled, patient, always respectful of its readers
but always unafraid, is quickly indignant at injustice; is
unswayed by the appeal of privilege or the clamor of the
mob; seeks to give every man a chance and, as far as law
and honest wage and recognition of human brotherhood
can make it so, an equal chance; is profoundly patriotic
while sincerely promoting international good will and

cementing world-comradeship; is a journalism of humanity, of and for today's world.

CHAPTER 14

Full text of Tribune's press release announcing its Chapter 11 filing:

Tribune Company to Voluntarily Restructure Debt Under Chapter 11

Publishing, Interactive and Broadcasting Businesses
   to Continue Operations
Chicago Cubs and Wrigley Field Not Part of
   Chapter 11 Filing; Monetization Efforts to Continue

CHICAGO, December 8, 2008—Tribune Company today announced that it is voluntarily restructuring its debt obligations under the protection of Chapter 11 of the U.S. Bankruptcy Code in the United States Bankruptcy Court for the District of Delaware. The company will continue to operate its media businesses during the restructuring, including publishing its newspapers and running its television stations and interactive properties without interruption, and has sufficient cash to do so.

The Chicago Cubs franchise, including Wrigley Field, is not included in the Chapter 11 filing. Efforts to monetize the Cubs and its related assets will continue.

"Over the last year, we have made significant progress internally on transitioning Tribune into an entrepreneurial company that pursues innovation and stronger ways of serving our customers," said Sam Zell, chairman and CEO of Tribune. "Unfortunately, at the same time, factors beyond our control have created a perfect storm—a precipitous decline in revenue and a tough economy coupled with a credit crisis that makes it extremely difficult to support our debt.

"We believe that this restructuring will bring the level of our debt in line with current economic realities, and will take pressure off our operations, so we can continue to work toward our vision of creating a sustainable, cutting-edge media company that is valued by our readers, viewers and advertisers, and plays a vital role in the communities we serve. This restructuring focuses on our debt, not on our operations."

The company filed today for Court approval of various, customary First-Day Motions, including: maintaining employee payroll and health benefits; the fulfillment of certain pre-filing obligations; the continuation of the Tribune's cash management system; the ability to honor all customer programs. The company anticipates its First-Day Motions will be approved in the next few days.

While the company has sufficient cash to continue operations, to supplement its cash availability in the event of even more significant declines in its operating results, the company has negotiated an agreement with Barclays to maintain post-filing its existing securitization facility. Barclays has also agreed to provide a letter of credit facility. The company expects to submit these agreements to the Court for approval as part of its First-Day Motions.

Since going private last year, Tribune has re-paid approximately $1 billion of its senior credit facility. During this time, the company has been rewriting the business model for its media assets with the goal of building a sustainable, innovative, competitive company that provides relevant products for its customers and communities.

For further information on Tribune Company's Chapter 11 filing, please visit *Tribune.com* or *http://chapter11 .epiqsystems.com/tribune*, or call 888-287-7568. The company will provide updates regarding ongoing operations plans as they become available.

NOTES

Prologue

1. Sam Zell, in conversation with the author, August 8, 1996.
2. CNBC interview, December 10, 2008.
3. Stanley Ross, in conversation with the author, November 11, 2008.

Chapter 1. Little Blue Pill

1. *Los Angeles Times* meeting, February 8, 2008.
2. Ashland University speech, October 14, 2004.
3. *Dividend* magazine, University of Michigan Stephen M. Ross School of Business, Spring 2006.
4. Ashland University speech, October 14, 2004.

Chapter 2. A "Different" Sort

1. *Dividend* magazine, University of Michigan Stephen M. Ross School of Business, Spring 2006.
2. "Chicago Tonight," WTTW-TV, Rich Samuels.
3. *Dividend,* Spring 2006.
4. Ibid.
5. "Chicago Tonight," WTTW-TV, Rich Samuels.

6. *Dividend,* Spring 2006.
7. Ashland University speech, October 14, 2004.

Chapter 3. Grave Dancer

1. Sam Zell, in conversation with the author, October 8, 1996.
2. Ibid.
3. Ibid.

Chapter 4. Edifice Rex

1. Stephanie Strom, "A Rockefeller Center Infusion of $250 Million," *New York Times,* August 17, 1995.
2. Rockefeller Center Properties Inc. statement, August 15, 1995.
3. Stephanie Strom, "A 'Vulture' Looks Skyward," *New York Times,* September 10, 1995.
4. Ibid.
5. Ibid.
6. Letter from Sam Zell to Peter Linneman, October 5, 1995.
7. Peter Linneman, in conversations with the author, October 30, 2008, and November 18, 2008.

Chapter 5. Equitable Arrangements

1. Equity Lifestyle Properties Inc., 2007 annual report.
2. Equity Office Properties quarterly conference call, September 15, 1997.
3. Sam Zell, in conversation with the author, October 8, 1996.
4. Ashland University speech, October 14, 2004.
5. *National Real Estate Investor,* August 2001.
6. Ibid.
7. Bloomberg News, October 13, 2004.
8. "Zell: REIT Pricing, Privatization to Go on 5 More Years," Dow Jones Newswires, November 29, 2006.

Chapter 6. Bidding War

1. University of Michigan speech, September 21, 2007.
2. "A Bidding War Between Egos at Blackstone Group and Vornado," *New York Times,* February 8, 2007.
3. University of Michigan speech, September 21, 2007.
4. Ibid.

Chapter 7. Sam's Way (or the Highway)

1. Jonathan Kempner, in conversation with the author, August 4, 2008.
2. Ashland University speech, October 14, 2004.
3. Ibid.
4. Kevin Roderick, in conversation with the author, December 2, 2008.
5. Peter Linneman, in conversations with the author, October 30, 2008, and November 18, 2008.
6. Stephen Quazzo, in conversation with the author, August 22, 2008.
7. Randy Rowe, in conversation with the author, August 21, 2008.
8. Ashland University speech, October 14, 2004.

Chapter 8. Open Kimono

1. Tribune Co., May 19, 2005.
2. Securities & Exchange Commission filing, June 13, 2006.
3. Tribune Co., June 14, 2006.
4. "Zell Wins Tribune in Bid to Revive a Media Empire," *Wall Street Journal*, April 3, 2007.

Chapter 9. Newspaper Neophyte

1. "Zell exec believes in papers; Member of family with publishing roots calls woes overstated," *Chicago Tribune*, James Rainey, May 10, 2007.
2. Ibid.
3. *Chicago Tribune* interview, December 22, 2007.
4. Corey Rosen, in conversation with the author, October 17, 2008.
5. *Wall Street Journal*, December 20, 2007.
6. Tribune Co. interview, December 22, 2007.

Chapter 10. Paper Tiger

1. *Los Angeles Times* meeting, February 8, 2008.
2. Nathaniel Popper, "Billionaire Boychiks Battle for Media Empire," *Jewish Daily Forward*, April 13, 2007.
3. Ibid.
4. Lauren Rich Fine, in conversation with the author, November 17, 2008.
5. Ibid.
6. Dean Mills, in conversation with the author, October 2, 2008.
7. Tribune Co. press conference, December 20, 2007.
8. Tribune Co. interview, December 22, 2007.
9. Tribune staff meeting, February 8, 2008.

10. Ibid.
11. Ibid.
12. Tribune Co. quarterly conference call, June 2008.
13. Tribune Co. corporate statement, March 11, 2008.

Chapter 11. Nonconformist

1. Tribune Co., April 1, 2008.
2. Ashland University speech, October 14, 2004.
3. Tribune Co. meeting, February 8, 2008.
4. *Chicago Tribune* interview, December 22, 2007.
5. Ibid.
6. Tribune Co. meeting, February 8, 2008.
7. Tribune Co. statement, September 22, 2008.
8. Tribune Co. press release, September 17, 2008.
9. Press release from law firm Cotchett, Pitre & McCarthy, September 17, 2008.
10. Peter Linneman, in conversations with the author, October 30, 2008, and November 18, 2008.
11. Jonathan Kempner, in conversation with the author, August 4, 2008.
12. UCLA Armand Hammer Museum of Art and Cultural Center speech, Los Angeles, February 21, 2008.
13. Stanley Ross, in conversation with the author, November 11, 2008.

Chapter 12. Revolt

1. Tribune Co. meeting, February 19, 2008.
2. Ibid.
3. Ibid.
4. CNBC interview, June 27, 2008.
5. Lauren Rich Fine, in conversation with the author, November 13, 2008.
6. Peter Linneman, in conversations with the author, October 30, 2008, and November 18, 2008.
7. University of Chicago, Executive MBA program speech, June 8, 2007.
8. Lauren Rich Fine, in conversation with the author, November 13, 2008.
9. Kevin Roderick, in conversation with the author, December 2, 2008.

Chapter 13. Fire Sale

1. *Chicago Tribune* interview, December 22, 2007.
2. Tribune Co. meeting, February 8, 2008.
3. News Corp. conference call, May 7, 2008.

4. Inland Press Association speech, October 22, 2007.
5. "Cubs Sale Not Expected by Opening Day," MLB.com, January 19, 2008.
6. Ibid.
7. CNBC appearance, June 27, 2008.
8. *Chicago Tribune* interview, December 22, 2007.
9. Ibid.
10. "L.A. Times Names Eddy Hartenstein to Publisher's Post," *Los Angeles Times*, August 16, 2008.
11. CNBC appearance, June 27, 2008.

Chapter 14. Failure *Is* an Option

1. Tribune Co. press release, December 8, 2008.
2. CNBC interview, December 10, 2008.
3. U.S. Justice Department complaint, December 9, 2008.
4. Tribune Co., December 9, 2008.
5. Tribune Co. press conference, December 20, 2007.
6. CNBC interview, December 10, 2008.

Chapter 15. Professional Opportunist

1. Stephen Siegel, in conversation with the author, September 22, 2008.
2. Peter Linneman, in conversations with the author, October 30, 2008, and November 18, 2008.
3. Bloomberg Television, October 24, 2008.
4. Equity International, July 28, 2008.
5. Keynote Address, Urban Land Institute Latin America Conference, October 27, 2008.
6. Bloomberg Television, October 24, 2008.
7. Ibid.
8. Knowledge@Wharton Real Estate in Emerging Markets Forum, January 19, 2009.
9. Ashland University speech, October 14, 2004.

Epilogue

1. DLA Piper Real Estate Summit, September 23, 2008.
2. Ibid.
3. Ibid.

Appendix

Chapter 8: Securities & Exchange Commission filing, June 10, 2006.
Chapter 9: Tribune Co. press release, April 7, 2007.
Chapter 10: Walter Williams, "The Journalists' Creed," University of Missouri
School of Journalism.
Chapter 14: Tribune Co. press release, December 8, 2008.

INDEX